Respect

in the *family*

To order additional copies of *Respect in the Family,*
by Marilyn A. Wolcott, call 1-800-765-6955.

Visit us at www.rhpa.org
for more information on Review and Herald products.

Respect
in the *family*

Marilyn A. Wolcott

R

REVIEW AND HERALD® PUBLISHING ASSOCIATION
HAGERSTOWN, MD 21740

The author assumes full responsibility for the accuracy of all facts and
quotations as cited in this book.

This book was
Edited by Eugene Lincoln
Cover design and illustration by GenesisDesign/Bryan Gray
Typeset: 11/15 Times

PRINTED IN U.S.A.

03 02 01 00 99   5 4 3 2 1

R&H Cataloging Service
Wolcott, Marilyn A.   1950-
    Respect in the family.

    1. Family life.   2. Respect.   I. Title.

        306.87

ISBN 0-8280-1337-3

Contents

with careful planning and a large dose of creativity, tempered with lots of prayer, we can effectively aim our children toward acceptable behaviors.

Introduction

My four children are not "perfect" in any sense of the word. They have quarreled, don't always do their chores, skipped classes, sulked, colored on living room walls, not always arrived home on schedule—you know, the normal things children do in most homes. Towels left on the bathroom floor and beds unmade. And yet, we do have something special between us that overrides these "normal" behaviors.

And it certainly isn't because I am anything close to a "perfect" parent. I make more serious mothering blunders than I would ever be able to describe or even admit; and yet, despite my failings, I benefit from an unusual sense of respect and companionship with my children. I screamed when I should have remained silent. I badgered when I should have been accepting. I talked to friends on the phone when I should have been listening to my children. I made unrealistic demands in some cases. But nearly always I knew where the children were and what they were doing—and I rarely set a curfew, because they liked to come home.

One week a few years ago I received several questions from people in our church and school asking for my "secret" for raising such *good* kids. It started me thinking about the strengths and struggles of our family. I really didn't have any answers.

As I continued to ponder the questions of these fellow parents, I decided to ask the people who were the resident authorities on our family. I first asked the questions of the children individually. "What makes our family unique?" And "Do you think we're different from other families?" I don't remember any exact answers; except for Krista's answer. And I remember her response because at that moment in our relationship, things were rocky. She was in the full throes of adolescence and stubborn independence from Mom and family. We disagreed often.

In essence, she replied, "I have no idea why we're different, but we are, and I think you should figure it out and write a book about it, because I am certainly going to need to read it in case I ever have kids." (Most of the time she had asserted she would never have children because she didn't like babies, but I took it with the same grain of salt as I had heard her proclamations against boyfriends a few years previous!)

Later we discussed the topic in family worship, and I listened with wonder as all four of the children stated adamantly that my assignment was to define the reasons for our pleasant and successful relationships. Further, it would then be my task to put down my discoveries in a *series* of books about family relationships. I felt humble in the face of their praise of my ability to be their mother, but also highly complimented because I knew their comments didn't stem from my actions but from something much bigger.

Somehow they had grasped the presence of Jesus in my life. No matter what fool thing I did, they knew I loved them beyond description, and I still had credibility. I had shown them the unconditional love that can be attributed only to heavenly sources. Behavior and actions have not preserved our family, but it is the underlying love and acceptance that carries us past all the intrusions and upsets. As a family we have endured some shameful experiences, and together we have faced the consequences. We've held each other accountable and created an environment allowing for personal change.

Our biggest public shame came when my pastor husband and the children's previously devoted father left his family and ministry. It felt as if the whole world watched as we stumbled painfully toward a new life and a new sense of purpose. I understood the scarlet letter. I, too, felt branded and labeled. What sort of wife would cause her husband to take off? Together the children and I learned to hold our heads high once again. We drew close to each other and learned to lean completely on Jesus and to trust Him in everything. And we learned that a great strength is to be found in family unity. Together we regained our self-respect and rebuilt our mutual respect.

A while ago I visited with a neighbor, also the mother of four children, and she commented how glad she was to have them all in school now, and she wished the school day could be longer. I felt sad for her. *Parenting should be fun and satisfying.* I kept pondering what was missing in my neighbor's home that I found within my own home.

My children have now gone on to college and left home, and one of them has married. I've had more time to reflect on the explanation for the special relationship the children and I continue to enjoy. The pleasure they find in each other's company and with me is a treat and treasure to all of us, but especially to me, their mother. To have my children enjoy each other gives me a lot of inner joy and peace, a sense of a job well done.

And now as I begin the business of setting down my discoveries on paper, I feel humble all over again. I am grateful for the opportunity to be a mother. I appreciate the patience and perseverance of these children who have taught me how to be a mother. Parenting is not a skill that you can learn or develop until you're suddenly caught in the middle of it.

I continue to make blunders in the ever-changing role of mom to young adults, yet my children continue to like me. And I think I'm finally beginning to understand the reason they regard me so highly.

It all began when I gave them respect: Respect for their feelings, however foolish or immature. Respect for their individuality within the context of a large family. Respect for their dignity in front of family members and friends. Respect for their need to be children, and now, respect for them as young adults with beliefs sometimes different from my own.

The source of this respect comes from the value I have received from my Father in Heaven—the Father who sent His own Son to this dangerous and wicked world on my behalf. When I begin to understand how valuable I am to God; when I begin to acknowledge the companionship of the Holy Spirit no matter how pitiful my life at any given moment; when I catch a glimpse of heaven and my significance in its light, my self-respect flourishes. A person with a healthy dose of self-respect automatically respects other people.

And this is the basis of the many things I have learned. It is first a spiritual journey and second a parenting journey. The quality and consistency of my parenting will be reflected by the quality and consistency of my walk with God. So, while the words of this book will be primarily about the lessons I have learned—lessons taught by my four children—the foundation for my ability to learn those lessons is based on my desire to be like Him.

I invite you to relive that journey with me through the chapters of this book. I will give you examples from the pages of our family diary and from the experiences of friends who have walked the journey with me. But I promise my children and my friends to protect their identity when necessary and to give you a true story in a camouflaged setting from time to time. Most of all, I will respect you, my readers, by sharing only from the depths of my heart, and I will treat your time with the respect I believe you deserve.

Chapter 1

Respecting Our Mates

U ncle Fred, a research chemist, commands honor and respect while at work in his job. His interests, hobbies, and professional abilities far overshadow most of the people in our little world. But Uncle Fred does not have the respect of his wife, his three children, and his grandchildren. He plays the role of resident buffoon. His wife may poke fun at the way he dresses, and always reminds him of forgotten details. His children join in her ridicule. And now the grandchildren have added their jokes. Good-natured Uncle Fred accepts all their put-downs with obvious good humor and adds his own. He knows he will never measure up. His self-esteem fails to match his talents and abilities.

Whenever our families visit, my children come home feeling troubled about the lack of respect Uncle Fred receives from his entire family. And the children believe his wife bears the blame. They have discussed it thoroughly and think that if Aunt Molly started speaking to Uncle Fred with more open support, their children and their families would treat Uncle Fred better.

Joan, a young mother with three small children, feels overwhelmed. She wipes noses, gets drinks, settles squabbles, and changes diapers all day long. She manages to get supper on the table and keep the house at least clean enough to ward off the health department. She's tired and stressed, and she feels very unappreciated. The highlight of her day comes when her husband walks through the door. Phew! Help at last!

He collapses in the recliner chair, thumbs through the mail, and opens the evening paper. The children climb over his lap and romp at his feet. Joan ignores the children's needs and concentrates on the kitchen, Mark can take care of them now. But Mark doesn't know about this assignment. He's glad to be off his feet for a few minutes and just to relax before dinner. The kids are fun, and it's so cute that they like to climb on him while he reads, but he doesn't notice runny noses and doesn't even hear their little quarrels.

This arrangement can be only a prelude to trouble. One of the biggest problems in any marriage relationship comes from unmet expectations. Joan does not discuss her decision to assign Mark to child-care immediately upon his arrival home. She just assumes that now he will help her out. Mark doesn't know Joan has made this decision and thinks that she is capable of handling whatever the children need, so why should he worry about it?

Rather than address this issue openly, both of them exchange barbs back and forth at dinner. Or perhaps when one of the children asks Joan for something, she will say, "Go ask your father." And the children become go-betweens for a cold war that no one understands. Without identifying the problem, it will escalate into a deep freeze, and the respect between Joan and Mark will be completely gone.

To show affection to someone that you honestly believe neglects his or her share of the parenting responsibilities can be more than difficult. Mark gets tired of being the bad guy, so he snipes back whenever Joan makes a catty remark. If you were to ask either Joan or Mark why they are acting this way, they probably would not be able to give you an answer.

Respect between a husband and wife can be a fragile and illusive quality. But it is absolutely essential if we are to give our children a foundation for their own self-worth. When Mommy doesn't show respect and treat Daddy with dignity, can she really expect the children to do so? When Daddy doesn't treat Mommy with honor, why should anyone else treat her that way?

The Bible contains some verses that are often treated with disdain and avoided. But I think these verses give us the only real answer to this dilemma of parental respect.

"Wives, submit to your husbands as to the Lord. . . . Husbands, love your wives, just as Christ loved the church and gave himself up for her" (Ephesians 5:22-25, NIV).

These words can be scary. One reason we dislike these verses stems from the misuse and misapplications that many of us have witnessed. Another reason we are frightened by them is that they demand we remove all the barriers between us. As long as each of us needs to defend ourselves from the other, we cannot truly submit. And to love another as God loves me, wow! That's commitment. Am I willing to make a decision based on my wife's best good rather than on what I think is my own best good? If I don't defend me, who will? The scripture says your wife will honor you. But it's pretty risky to submit yourself to someone who doesn't love you with the same unselfish love as God.

Every married couple will have to wrestle these concepts out for themselves. It's an ongoing process and not something on which you make a decision today and then forget. It's not a popular attitude in today's world of women's liberation, but I believe it is essential to the foundation we set in our homes for our children to feel safe, loved, and valued. How can a child feel safe if Mommy doesn't feel safe?

Family counselors can show us the reactions of children whenever they live in a home of marital strife. Children instinctively feel they are the source of the problem. If Daddy doesn't come home anymore, the child wants to know why Daddy is mad at him. If Mommy cries a lot, the child wants to know how he can make her happy again. A child is the center of his own world, and when things go wrong, he blames himself and believes he can do something to change it.

When a child doesn't see parents give respect to each other, he begins to feel that it no longer matters whether or not that parent is obeyed. When a child disobeys, he loses self-respect. A child without self-respect disobeys more and more. So a no-win cycle begins. That cycle can really be stopped only when the child sees that the parents are worthy of his respect. A respected parent can inspire obedience and give the child an atmosphere of confidence and security.

One home that we have visited many times has one respected parent and one dishrag parent. The children snap to attention and respond immediately to the respected parent, and they completely ignore and do not seem to hear the words of the other parent. It's an amazing difference to watch. The verdict is still out on how this will affect those children in the long term, but it has already affected their ability to respond to others in authority. Teachers of the same gender of the respected parent experience no difficulty in the classroom. But teachers of the same gender as the spineless parent cannot seem to catch the attention of the children.

One writer a long time ago wrote, "The most important gift a father can give to his children is to truly love their mother." I agree, though I would like to add that it works both ways.

In the situations I have cited, these mothers and fathers, husbands and wives, happen to be people who have truly loved each other and who truly want what is best for their children. But they have gotten trapped in the routines of daily life and have gotten caught up in destructive cycles without even realizing it. Anyone can get caught in this cycle.

A newlywed wife told me recently that she discovered she and her beloved husband could probably live together and become totally separate people because they are both so driven and busy in their own careers. In addition, they have some pretty definite ideas on which they don't always agree, so it's easier to avoid letting those disagreements become issues. When they discovered this was happening in their marriage, they made a choice and a commitment to remain a team and to deal with those disagreeable issues. They made a choice to make time for each other and to treat each other with respect even when they didn't agree.

This decision will have to be repeated over and over. And they will still find that sometimes they have drifted and will have to go back and start all over yet again. But they've made the right start.

Other friends whose children have just married and left home are discovering that they really don't even know each other anymore. After years of focusing on the children, they now have only each other and aren't quite sure where to go from here. Marriage consists of lots of decisions to put the husband and wife first. When the children receive more attention than the marriage the balance is tilted and very off center. This will always be true: Loving your mate is the very best gift you can give your children.

But what to do when there is no longer a mate? In today's single-parent world, that is a serious problem. It was a problem in our household too.

To begin to deal with this, single parents must address initially the improvement of their own self-respect. Any loss of a marriage partner, whether through death or divorce, can be damaging to anyone's self-esteem. We can be diligent in punishing ourselves. So, as single parents, it's imperative that we do things actively to rebuild that sense of self-worth.

As I mentioned in the Introduction, this self-esteem comes first from recognizing how much God loves you. Start there. Spend time with God in Bible study. Spend time with God in music. Spend time with God in any of the multitude of books with other people's testimonies about Him. Spend time with God in prayer. Just spend time with Him until you realize again how very much He loves you. And while you are discovering God's love for you, you will discover also that this same God loves your children far more than you will ever be able to. So you will also learn to trust your children to His care.

The second most important thing you can do is to surround yourself with friends who treat you well. I highly recommend that you develop two-parent families as friends whenever possible. This will give your children the example of husband-wife interactions, and they will see the opposite parent in a role of support and of authority. Encourage these friends to support you to your children and to let your children's respect for their parent be reinforced. This will make a far bigger difference than you probably will ever be able to measure.

Third, share your achievements with your children. Let them know when you have accomplished something special. Invite them to celebrate with you. Family celebrations contribute a lot to an individual's self-worth and sense of specialness. One mother who went back to college to develop a career to support her family always posted her good grades on the fridge right along with her children's school papers. She also posted and shared term papers and final exams with good grades.

Another way of sharing achievements is whenever you receive a promotion or a raise at work, give the children evidence of it. Let them in on the recognition you receive from others in your adult world. This will give them a bigger picture of who you are and will help them to set goals of whom they want to become.

The issue of divorce presents a serious challenge in the assignment of respect to the absent parent. Some of these absent parents really are scoundrels. Some are just plain absent. Some play table tennis with the children. In every case, emotions run higher and deeper than anyone ever knew they could. All of us are capable of things we never knew about ourselves—things that scare us even now just to think about. And children are often the true victims in this emotional war.

Shortly before my own divorce I became friends with a woman who had been divorced and remarried. I later realized that God put this woman in my path to prepare me for the years that lay ahead. She shared many philosophies with me about how she had related to her children throughout her divorce and into her second marriage. She gave me more good counsel than I could share in one book.

She made a decision that her children needed to respect their father in spite of the mess he had made of their lives. She determined that they would not hear one critical or demeaning comment about him from her lips. She also decided that she wouldn't hide his faults or deny them, but the children would learn the truths for themselves, not from her. That's a noble mother. And I learned from my own experience how very difficult that can be. But a friend paid me a compliment a little while ago. She said that my children must have been nearly in their teens before they knew all the circumstances of our divorce.

The flip side of this issue is that when children lose respect for one of their parents, they lose respect also for the parent who chose to be married to someone unworthy of respect. Hmm. Think about that. Was my discernment so poor that I couldn't judge husband material any better than that? Is that what we want our children to think?

A mother who raised her children alone led them to believe their father had been a war hero. In reality he sat in prison for life. When questioned about her deception to her children, she responded, "I had to make a decision to give them a good example to replicate or a bad example. I chose to give them inspiration."

I'm not suggesting we tell our children untruths but rather that we give them the most positive example we can, rather than listing all the absent parent's faults. This is a choice we single parents will always have to make. Do we want our children to build their self-worth on a no-account person or on someone of value?

I chose to focus on telling my children about the man I married. I don't know about him now, and what he chose to become later didn't really enter into my discussions with the children. At the time I married him I believed him to be a good person with high standards and abilities. When my children emulated a part of him that was positive, I told them so. When they copied another part of him, I chose to hold my comments for a private chat with a friend.

Through the years, as the children have grown up, they have learned for themselves that their father was not perfect. They've been hurt and disappointed. No one makes excuses for him, but neither have they been destroyed by it. They know that once he was a good husband and father. They also know that there is only one Source of power for anyone to be a good husband or wife and father or mother: dependence on God. Away from God we have no guarantee that any of us will be all that we should be to the people who love and depend on us.

Chapter 2

Maintaining Dignity

Alvin, my 14-year-old son, and I strolled across the park, chatting amiably. The brassy shouts of the woman sitting nearby on the park bench blared into our conversation and thoughts. We halted and couldn't help staring. She sat on the bench shoving a lap full of projects into her bag. She continued to yell to a group of children playing across the field.

We looked over at the children to see their response. They continued to play, disregarding the threats. I couldn't imagine being able to play contently with such a barrage of noise aimed at me. Though I felt annoyed at the intrusion into our pleasant conversation, as a mother I remembered the rebuff of sometimes being ignored by my own children when I called them.

As these thoughts and emotions swept through me, my son muttered quietly, "I wouldn't come either if you talked to me that way."

Something lit within my mind. All these years I felt and saw how parents must feel when their children disobey and act out in a public setting. What I had failed to consider was how a child would feel when his parent talked and acted inappropriately in front of others. If I am embarrassed when my immature child throws a fit in the grocery store, how much more embarrassing it must feel to be dependent on an adult who throws tantrums.

As we walked away I was appalled at the idea that perhaps this mother did not even think her words and attitude to be a problem. After all, she's the mom; it's the job of children to obey. I doubt if she gave her words and tone a thought as she continued to berate her playing children.

My son's words and insight haunted me for days, and I began to carefully consider the messages I gave to my children. Did I take them out for misbehaving in church and then make a scene while scolding them? Did I frown and glare every time one of them said or did something unmannerly? What tone of voice did I use when I asked them to do a chore?

I recall the time I answered the phone and spoke more politely to a total stranger than I had been speaking to my daughter moments before. Her wistful observation, "Mom, I wish you talked to me in your telephone voice," struck clear to my heart. What hit me hardest was how I was feeling when I spoke those two different ways. I made an exciting discovery that should have been obvious long before now. *Screaming parents do not feel good about themselves.* Consequently, children being screamed at are very unlikely to feel good about their parent or about themselves either.

A parent who loses control—whether in private or in public—gives the child several messages. First, the parent tells all who watch him that he doesn't like himself very much. Second, he broadcasts his inability to maintain discipline over his own words and actions. Third, and worst of all, the little ones being addressed with such tones begin to feel they must not be very good people. They start to wonder, "What's wrong with me?"

The child is dependent on this out-of-control grown-up to navigate the big scary world, so the child may get frightened. A frightened child becomes unpredictable and may further complicate an explosive situation.

The tone of voice we use when we speak to our children reflects not only our emotional state of mind but also our level of respect. I began to realize that when we possess self-respect, we speak and act differently toward others. When I truly value other people and recognize them as individuals worthy of God's love and salvation, I automatically speak more politely to them. Sometimes people do not think of young children in the same way that they consider adults. Big mistake! These children are simply little people and are even more precious in the sight of heaven because of their innocence. However, these "little people" can sometimes push every one of our aggravation buttons, and consideration is the last thing on our minds. All our negative emotions are aroused. I wish we could have been provided a warning light to flash whenever we're on the verge of losing control! When this happens, it's important to keep our voice calm. This will help to keep our emotions calm, too. We then make it much easier for them to want to cooperate with our requests. A child obeying his parents likes himself much more than the child who doesn't. So, in addition to allowing our children to respect their parents, we also give them a measure of self-respect. This all becomes a cycle of honor and dignity.

Let's go back and look at our opening scene. The mother sits at the park bench doing her own activity. That's fine. The mother decides it's time to go home. That's Ok. The problem begins when the mother tries to attract the attention of her children while she also tries to collect her own things, and she doesn't want to waste a moment of time.

Suppose the mother carefully collects her things into her bag and then quickly walks over to the place her children are playing. They will undoubtedly notice her approach and will be prepared to hear her message of "time to go." Because she's now standing very near to where the children play, she doesn't have to raise her voice, and she can talk to them in a quiet and controlled tone. Also, because her things are collected and she's on her feet, she's giving them the additional message of "I am ready to go right now, so hurry." An extra thoughtful gesture might be to give the children a verbal three-minute warning. This gives them time to make a mental adjustment and to wind down or time to finish their game. In doing this the mother tells her children that she respects their activity and recognizes that the child has equal importance.

The secondary benefit of this approach touches my son and me as we enjoy our own walk through the park. Our ears and conversation are spared the uncomfortable sounds and attitudes. So our time and space receive her respect as a by-product.

Another incident I witnessed still jars my thoughts. A harried young mother with a baby and preschooler locked her keys in the car. Her frustration level obviously had soared beyond normal before this event happened, so the locked-up keys probably pushed her over her breaking point. Immediately she began shaking and belittling the preschooler for locking the keys in the car. I sat inside at my desk and tried to think what I could do. Her treatment of the little boy appeared so severe as to suggest someone's calling the police or child protection services. I felt reluctant to intervene but was sure that my failure to do so might result in injury to the boy. I invited her into the office to use my phone and hoped that the changed environment would give her time to gather herself together.

It is not uncommon for people to project their frustrations onto their family members, but commonness does not mean it is proper. It's much easier for a person with self-respect to take responsibility for her own action. This young mother could have already been insecure; or perhaps she had recently had a fight with her husband and he had told her she couldn't do anything right. Then she locked the keys in the car and proved him right. Well, that hurt too bad to think about, so it must be someone else's fault the keys got locked in the car.

All of us choose to develop and protect our own self-worth. Parents bear the extra responsibility of providing an atmosphere of respect for their children. Those who grow up in homes offering acceptance and confidence begin parenthood with some real advantages. But those who miss this opportunity as children have a double need to create a haven of assurance within their own homes so they can refill their own personal quotas of self-respect and then nurture this same sense of esteem in their children. Parents must first possess an inner sense of honor before they can pass it on to their children.

Sadly, the ability to conceive a child does not automatically endow anyone with the ability to parent that same child. I have discovered that the art of becoming a parent is a lifelong process, rather than a course we can take in college and pass with As and Bs. There's no final exam and no graduation. We can choose to stay trapped in the morass of the problems we inherited from our own parents, or we can choose to give our children a better heritage.

For those who received "this gift" from their parents, praise God! Be prepared to pass it on to your own children.

Another far-too-familiar scene is that of the screaming mother and child in the grocery store. If it's embarrassing to us as unwilling onlookers and total strangers, imagine being the child in this situation. A toddler out of control does embarrass himself, but he lacks the maturity and self-control to recognize what to do once it's started. He certainly doesn't need help from his parents in adding to the embarrassment.

Though every scene situation is unique, one principle should prevail. As quickly and quietly as possible the parent should remove the child from the public eye. This might mean getting a screaming child out of a grocery store before you are finished shopping.

If your child loses his temper in the midst of a neighborhood softball game, quietly walk over to him and remove him to the house, the car, a big tree, or simply away from all the other children. Give him time to regain his composure before allowing him to return to the game. He may resist the action of removal, but later (maybe not until he has his own children) he will thank you for preserving what little dignity he had left at that moment.

A toddler pounding the floor and screaming can be given privacy simply by having his parent leave the room. The tantrum ends much sooner when there is no audience. Any parent trying to handle or talk to a child in the middle of a tantrum suddenly becomes a part of the struggle. When the parent leaves the room, the toddler has to have the tantrum all by himself, and that's not nearly as rewarding. The parent maintains not only his own self-respect, but also the respect of the child.

Parents who yell, lecture, or spank their children in front of others demean their children. They also demean themselves. Our job as parents is to stay in control and to do all we can to maintain our child's dignity and self-respect, regardless of how the child has behaved. If discipline is nec-essary when others are present, take the child into a private room and han-dle the matter behind closed doors. Your child is worth this extra effort—and so are you. By protecting your child's dignity and reputation you protect your own reputation also.

One of my sons has a good friend with whom he has spent many hours in his home. This boy's parents often have long tirades about various is-sues in the teen's life. My son has endured too many of these episodes and is very disgusted with the parents and embarrassed for his friend. Interestingly, I have also become disgusted with the parents, though I have never witnessed the scenes. Their reputation has been affected by their lack of discretion in front of their son's friends.

I have two cousins very close to my sister and me in age. We used to spend a week together every summer. My aunt made a serious impression on me as she managed to handle a significant number of misbehaviors in the course of a day. In all the time we stayed in their home, I never wit-nessed any discipline taking place. Oh, I knew that it did; it just happened quietly and privately. The offending child was removed from the main ac-tivity and dealt with away from any watching eyes. My aunt was a model for me as I dealt with my own difficult children.

My four children were born within a five-year period. Consequently, they are close in their allegiances as well as in their ages. The three older children all doted on their beloved baby brother. Whatever shortcomings he manifested, they were quick to counteract. Any time it became neces-sary for me to punish this charming little man, I received glaring expres-sions of contempt. The only way to be at all effective in handling the discipline of this family pet was for me to be sure that it was done in pri-vate. It does take extra effort to remove both you and the problem child, but it is effort that will be repaid into the next generation. Not only will the gift of respect that you give to your child be given back to you but it also will be passed on to your grandchildren.

Chapter 3

Delighting in Diversions

I collapsed on the couch in total exhaustion. Fortunately, I had collected a toy or two before I crashed, because only moments later the baby scampered across the room toward the overfilled wastebasket. I could almost see his thoughts as he crawled with definite purpose. I reached for the push toy and shoved it noisily into the room. Baby's attention was arrested by the toy, and he quickly changed direction to inspect this moving noisy object. Aha! Success! I could rest a few more minutes. Accidentally I had discovered an effective parenting technique: the art of diversion. When a child of any age heads in a direction that poses a problem to the child or to the family, quite often we can provide an applicable diversion to head off the problem situation before it begins. But it does take alert, involved, and creative parents to activate those diversions in just the right way. Let's begin with toddlers and babies.

As a new parent and an idealist, I had some extremely unreasonable expectations for the behavior of my children. My unwritten list of prescribed actions would have filled far too many columns. Somewhere

26

along my journey I learned to choose my issues and to keep them as simple as possible. I also learned that the best way to handle conflict with children is to avoid it. Some parents seem to generate conflict and disagreement, almost as a testimony to their own power and authority. But I hated it and accidentally discovered ways to minimize it. Real life seemed to offer more conflict than I wanted without my interference.

Some ways to avoid head-to-head scenes with small children are to keep their play area as child-ready as you can—but I don't suggest that all adult things be kept hidden. Just minimize them. Keep things to interest the child close at hand and use them to distract the child from the activities you don't want him or her to participate in (such as emptying waste baskets!). First of all, keep that wastebasket emptied often, so that if the toddler does explore its contents, he won't find much to spill. Second, be ready with an accepted activity rather than a "No! No!" And be realistic about the value of "things" in relationship to the value of a child. A priceless vase should not be kept where a child might be able to break it. But most of our belongings are not priceless and are worth much less than the heart of a child.

The only time I really punished a child for breaking something was when the child blatantly disobeyed my request to quit throwing things in the living room and broke a special vase. He refused to admit he had done something wrong: "It was just a dumb old vase." I cared about his attitude far more than the broken vase. But that's a different issue than a toddler breaking something special.

One friend had a little one who threw a tantrum whenever she needed to put his shoes or jacket on to go outside, or change his diapers or clothes. He hated to be interrupted in his play and would fuss and resist "No! No! No!" the entire time she dressed him. But she quietly did what needed to be done without any argument. She could have scolded or admonished him as I might have done, but she ignored his outburst and efficiently wrestled his shoes onto his feet. Another solution to such a problem might be to get easily donned shoes and clothes. One of my children wore cowboy boots for about three years while a preschooler. He hated to be bothered with shoestrings, velcro fasteners, or anything that slowed him down. It was easier just to buy him the boots, which slipped on and off without difficulty.

Again, avoid the conflicts that can be avoided. Choose the issues that matter and relax about the issues that simply cause stress to both parents and children. One parent could not convince her toddlers to stay out of the road. She tried spankings, threats, and always watching them, but she seemed unable to impress upon her youngest child the dangers of running into the street. One day while driving down the highway she saw an animal that had been hit by a car. With stomach churning, she stopped and got her children out of the car. She took each of them to view the massacred animal. She felt horrible about doing such a ghastly deed but her point was made, and the children quit venturing wrecklessly onto the roadways.

A phrase I read before the birth of my first child helped me to define my issues. A parent must "require prompt and perfect obedience" *(Child Guidance,* p. 86). Requiring prompt and strict obedience necessitates a lot of involvement from the parents. It means you are *never* off duty, whether at home, at church, or visiting friends. In light of such a serious responsibility, it's best to remember that the fewer the rules, the easier it is to enforce them.

In the beginning years of babyhood and toddlerhood, the important issues concerned the safety of the child and the people in the child's life. They were not allowed to participate in behavior that would hurt themselves or anyone else. Second, they were expected to follow my directives. I had to learn to minimize my requests, because my job was also to make sure that whatever I asked was obeyed. In the earliest years that meant doing the activity together.

For example, little children are usually quite eager to help, and they like to put their clothes away after they are folded on laundry days.

I naively assumed that the clothes traveling down the hall in little arms wound up near the clothes chest. Wrong. Shari would carry her bundles eagerly to the bedroom doors of the correct rooms and then toss the whole stack onto the floor and return to me smiling with accomplishment.

28

I learned through experience that if I didn't want to fold the same clothes several times, I needed to walk down the hall with her, watch, and help her to put them into the proper places.

When a parent requires prompt and exact obedience, he himself becomes involved in the activity of obeying, not just a body issuing orders.

As the children grow in ability and understanding the implementation of the requests begin to change—but the parent's involvement should not change. And beware, for your children may be smarter than you are! Mine all were. Each of them would be assigned a household chore. Some chores were completed with better quality than some others, and out of convenience, I tended to give the chores to the child who best fulfilled them. Thus I unknowingly rewarded the children who did the poorest job on their least favorite task, and the faithful child was punished because he got the hardest assignments.

Fortunately, I finally discovered their superior wisdom. I began to inspect completed jobs and to require a competence appropriate to the ability of the child. Some jobs were repeated several times before I checked them off the list as completed. But again, I was careful not to undermine the younger child who made the bed as well as he could. I straightened it after him when he wasn't watching, so I didn't discourage him from trying again. (Tip: During the younger years I made their beds with a fitted bottom sheet and washable comforter. One blanket can be much easier to straighten than several layers of bedding.)

Diversion is as effective in parenting preteen and teenagers as it is with toddlers. But it does take a serious commitment from both parents to be successful. A busy life with multiple scheduled activities becomes a natural diversion. A day full of responsibilities and challenges keeps a young person with lots of idle time from standing on street corners or hanging out in malls.

This issue was hard for me. We lived across the street from three teenage girls near the ages of my children. They attended public high school and didn't hold jobs or attend many after-school activities. They came home every day at 3:30 in the afternoon and were done for the day.

My children attended school and worked from 6:45 in the morning and didn't get home until after 7:00 in the evening. I often felt guilty about how busy they were, but later I realized that their busyness kept them from doing the things that caused many young people to wind up in trouble.

When teaching values to children, parents should start at a young age. Teach them to say no to drugs long before they encounter drugs. Bring them into contact with an unmarried teenage mother, and make sure they understand the consequences for the rest of the girl's life.

Create situations to address the serious issues and decisions your children will face. Include books and movies that present stories of wise choices and also examples showing the consequences of unwise behaviors. Continue to use real-life illustrations and offer evaluations of long-term results for the people involved. As you go through the process of just living your life, watch for the teachable moments. Remember to keep your comments succinct. Long speeches become lectures and usually leave a negative aftertaste, so check yourself before you say too much.

Also, be sure they understand that these decisions are not made while sitting on a hill overlooking the city on a moonlit night alone in a car with their special friend. The important decisions are always made long before the situation occurs. But it's up to us to prepare our children to deal with the tough issues *before* they meet them with and from friends.

By staying involved in your children's world you will also stay aware of the people and activities that involve them. Rather than telling them you don't like their friends, help them invite friends you do like. Help them plan activities you support and encourage. If an event is coming that you are uncomfortable with, arrange a way to attend it as a family—or get a family that shares your values to attend and be aware of your child.

Parenting teens and preteens is not a passive activity. This is probably not a good time for a parent to decide to go back to school and build a whole new life for himself. It's also not a good time for young people to come home from school to an empty house. Empty houses create atmospheres of artificial freedom.

In a recent newspaper editorial Ellen Goodman addressed the issue of after-school care for children of all ages. She cited statistics showing that the most fertile time for a teenage girl was after school in an empty house. For a variety of reasons, I feel that teenagers probably need even more parenting than toddlers. Statistics like that support my instincts.

I know several families that have made decisions and commitments to develop family group activities involving the entire family and keeping everyone active, busy, and healthy. This is a good way to prepare the family unit to meet the teen years as a team rather than sending their children off to grow up all alone in a scary world.

One family I know explored the logging country on motorbikes every weekend. Another family moved into the country and got involved with horses and trail rides. Another family bought a boat for waterskiing—and it went to the lake only when the entire family went together. Other friends started roller-blading. And another family group became avid international bird watchers with lists of the birds they have seen. Find an interest that captures the attention of the whole family and continue to engage in it throughout the child's transition into adulthood. It will provide many memories, many hours of satisfaction, and a terrific diversion from other less-wholesome activity; and it will connect the family to each other. Also, since we live in a world with so much inactivity, it will help to keep the family exercising together and maintain health and fitness.

But the question I hear you asking now is "what does all this diversion have to do with family respect?" Lots.

A great deal of energy and attention is invested in providing healthy diversions for all age groups of children. That energy spent on behalf of our children demonstrates our recognition of their worth. We don't spend this much energy on people who don't matter to us. It also shows that we parents place a high priority on our families. It's very difficult for a workaholic parent to invest this much time in the family, and when he does, he generates the respect of the children.

As I mentioned earlier, our children often are much wiser than we recognize. Wise children know when the parent values them and in turn they value and respect their parent much more. Consequently, we create an environment for trust and obedience as a natural outflowing of that respect. We parents must make it easy and natural for our children to want to obey us. When we make obedience a power struggle, we have given them a serious handicap. They might perform the action of obedience but lack the heart of obedience; and our real quest is to give our children the heart of obedience. By wanting to obey their parents, they also will learn to want to obey God.

And as they enjoy time spent with their families, perhaps they also will find it easier to want to spend time with God's larger family. When our children don't have a good picture of God, we should first look to ourselves and ask what picture of God we've given them. Do they see a family God who loves to spend time in their company, or do they see Him as a god who makes a list of rules of do's and don'ts?

When we avoid scenes that create dissension and lessen harmony, we protect our children's self-worth and maintain our own dignity. Most of us don't like ourselves after we have had a major disagreement with someone, much less someone whom we love. Peace, harmony, dignity, and personal value—what wonderful gifts to give our children. It's worth expending that additional energy. When we give our children these gifts, we also benefit from basking in that same peacefulness and accompanying harmony.

Chapter 4

Daunting
Discipline

Sheila angrily orders Tommy to the corner for a 10-minute time-out. He has sassed her for the umpteenth time today, and she's fed up. While Tommy sits and waits for the timer to ring and end his 10 minutes, Sheila lectures and storms around the room.

In many homes this scenario, or some variation of it, repeats itself numerous times each week. If we were to ask Sheila, she would explain that Tommy has been disciplined. But what has really happened would be that Mom was venting her emotions.

Discipline continues to be about the toughest subject for every parent; and yet few of us do a very good job of defining it. To many of us, discipline and punishment are synonymous. We have no clear goal of what that punishment or discipline is meant to accomplish, save a few moments of peace and perhaps a bit of revenge for having our authority challenged. I think we need to take a few steps outside ourselves once in a while and re-define the meaning of discipline and its purpose. We can easily get caught up in cycles of reacting and miss the intention of actions.

As parents our assignment is to provide a safe, nurturing environment while our children grow from babyhood to adulthood and to prepare them with the skills to handle life. So the goal of our discipline, in the first place, is to teach them to respond to our requests in order that they might be kept safe. The second goal is to teach them to conduct themselves in a responsible and appropriate manner with respect to the feelings and safety of those around them. The third goal is to give children the tools to become *self*-disciplined, to govern their emotions and their actions—to be controlled not by their feelings but rather by their brains.

Disciplining our children does not mean imposing of our wills, our moods, or our whims onto them. Some parents actually expect their children to do a lot of unreasonable things in order to prove that the parents control the household. Discipline becomes a power struggle and enforcement of authority rather than a training experience and positive development of personal control.

Punishment differs from discipline in that its main purpose is to inflict consequences as a negative motivation to change behavior. Some consequences occur as a natural result of certain actions. As parents, we instinctively protect our children from unpleasantness and we might be tempted to circumvent uncomfortable situations for our children. Don't do it!

At other times our job is to enact penalties for defiant or other unacceptable actions. Everything we do has some sort of result, and sometimes we bring serious retributions upon ourselves. Our children need to learn life lessons while they are young in order to live with positive rewards when they are older.

The ages of our children don't matter, the goals stay much the same. As our children grow in understanding and experience as well as years, we will vary our response to the methods of training them, but the goal should always be to teach them to be self-governed. Our ability to be successful in teaching this starts with the child's unquestionable confidence in us and his knowing exactly what to expect. Children need to know that we mean what we say and that we will do what we say we will do.

Earlier I mentioned the importance of the first three years of a child's life. In teaching obedience and the beginning of self-discipline, our effectiveness is essential. For the most part, teaching and enforcing obedience with a baby and toddler entails movement and physical implementation of our requests. That's the hardest part. To stay in the recliner chair and bark orders or to yell from the kitchen rather than washing and drying our hands and leaving our task to go to the child who needs instruction is easy. But in order to be effective in requiring obedience, we have to be mobile. And, these little ones are not going to grasp the significance of prolonged speeches and lectures, so keep the explanations brief and specific.

The children are playing outside on the swings and need to be inside and ready for supper in 15 minutes. Dad walks out to where they are playing and gives them a few pushes, and laughs and jokes with them for a few minutes. Then he suggests they go pick up their trucks and cars and put the Big Wheels away for the night before washing up for supper. Any activity undertaken together with a parent is much more likely to occur peacefully. Together Dad and children can wash up in the bathroom and be on hand to help serve up the meal. I agree this sounds idealistic, but I have witnessed at least one home where it is a typical scenario.

Or Dad could yell out to the children to quit playing, put stuff away, and come in for supper. I can almost guarantee that most children would not immediately cease their play and complete picking up before coming into the house.

Annie has been told three times to put her toys away and get ready for her evening bath. But she hasn't seemed to hear your words, so you start yelling. A better way to penetrate her imaginary play might be to approach her, crouch down, and put your hand on her shoulder before speaking. Many children have vivid imaginations and surprising powers of concentration. They actually do not recognize even that Mom or Dad is talking to them until the parents' voices have risen to shouting levels. Then everyone is mad. Try to avoid any possibility of being ignored or misunderstood. For the most part, a calm physical enforcement of your reasonable request—such as taking children gently by the hand, leading them in the desired task, or joining them to put toys away—may be all that's needed.

When a situation becomes out of control for the child, be very careful that you do not also get out of control. Children will probably hit out at other people, parents, siblings, or playmates. At some time children will scream and explode. What then? There's no right answer to this question, because no two children are alike. We will need to experiment to learn what effectively gives our child the motivation to change his behavior. But be careful *not* to condone unacceptable behavior with the excuse that it's normal for children this age.

Friends gave their 18-month-old child a spoonful of butter when he wanted it, saying they had read that it was normal for a child this age to like to eat plain butter. It's also normal for a child that age to hit a playmate over the head when he wants the toy the other child has. Normal does not mean acceptable.

The important thing to remember when administering punishment as a form of discipline is, first of all, to stay in calm control yourself, and the second is to make the punishment fit the "crime." When a toddler bonks someone over the head, you might lift him up and set him on a chair away from the play. Simply explain that he isn't allowed to hit other people and that he will not get to play for a few minutes. Set the timer and make sure the child sits on the chair without talking for the duration of the punishment. A general guideline for how long to sit out might be one minute for each year of age. In our household, a violation of the time-out (either talking or leaving the chair) meant simply that the timer was reset. One daughter wound up sitting out for a very long time one day since she couldn't last the full time without talking. Be careful not to argue with or lecture the child. Remember Sheila's example.

Another time I stood the children in the corner whenever they used inappropriate tones of voice or unacceptable words or attitudes. All it took was once for my daughter to know she couldn't bear to stand with her back to the others. In the future a glance or single reminder would improver her behavior instantly. But Michael needed numerous sessions in the corner. One day I overheard him telling an adult friend that it was good his face and nose were shaped right to fit corners well, since he spent so much time there!

But for one of my children I often felt like a child abuser at the end of the day. She required and seemed to ask specifically for several spankings and time-outs every day. When she grew older, she thanked me for caring enough about her bad attitude and frequent disobedience to stay with her through the journey to obedience and self-discipline. She also taught me the importance of a well-ordered household and a dependable schedule (which I will discuss in more detail later).

We hear much now about the need to avoid spanking children. I'm not going to add judgment about its rightness or wrongness. I did spank my children while they were little, and contrary to some writer's predictions, they did not see a spanking from a parent as permission to hit others. But whatever punishment you find it necessary to employ in disciplining your children, I believe a few basic principles are essential.

First, the punishment should be as private as is possible. In maintaining the child's privacy, you also maintain his dignity as well as your own.

Second, the parent should stay as calm and in control as possible. If you sense that you cannot stay in control, intervene in the activity but defer punishment until you can regain perspective. If a baby or young toddler pushes you to an out-of-control situation, you might possibly need some assistance in your own life. Don't be afraid to ask for help if you feel unreasonable anger or a vengeful spirit against your children. That does not mean you are a bad person but that you should seek help to change your own behavior and your own feelings. If you believe that your emotions are out of control or that your children might be in danger, do call a friend, a parent, a pastor, or a counselor. Don't wait.

To be a parent with young children is difficult, particularly if you are a single parent or a parent with a spouse who works long hours and is often away from home. Realizing that it's going to be hard, be sure to give yourself moments of luxury. That can be as simple as a soaking bubble bath after the children are in bed, a night out with friends, or a long chat on the phone with your mother. Whatever rejuvenates your spirit, make sure to include it into your life, no matter how hectic things seem. Also, be sure to get as much rest as you can and to maintain a healthy diet. In short, take good care of yourself and include some frequent pampering and rewards. You are the parent now, and no one else is going to take care of you.

Third, if you decide to spank your child, make sure that it's not a beating with dozens of hits. Two or three sharp swats on the bottom or thigh should be sufficient. Don't waste your energy on diaper-padded bottoms. Sometimes all you want is to startle or shock the child into paying attention. Be sure the action is appropriate to the extent of their misbehavior. One idea I learned suggested using spankings only for defiant acts of disobedience. We need to realize also that spankings should be used primarily on preschoolers. An older child will feel his dignity challenged and will be apt to react with rebellion and hate.

Fourth, be very sure that the child knows exactly what he did wrong. Always be specific and precise in communicating the expected behavior to your child. This means that if the activity spurs a spanking today, it should also incur a spanking tomorrow. If it's wrong this time, it must always be wrong.

As parents, one of our greatest challenges is to remain consistent in our treatment of our children. If sneaking food between meals is against the rules, and one child receives the consequence of missing the next meal, then all children should miss a meal for sneaking food. If you decide that uneaten food at one meal must first be eaten at the next meal, make sure you treat each occurrence the same.

The only exception of this would be the time you realize later that you overreacted and gave an inappropriate punishment. This discovery must prompt you to apologize and explain to all of your children that you regret your action. Also, assure them you have changed your mind about how this situation will be handled next time. Children will forgive you and continue to respect you, even when you make mistakes, *if you are honest with them.*

The one time I used a skipped supper as punishment wound up becoming a joke in our family memory banks. Second-grader Michael was to go to his room while the rest of us ate our meal. But as he left the room he spouted in anger, "You're going to feel bad when I'm dead in the morning!" And I guess the other three children believed him because he received three smuggled meals that night. Needless to say, I didn't use that penalty again.

Last, following whatever punishment you enact, always reassure your children of the complete forgiveness you offer and of your constant love for them. This is absolutely the most important ingredient of effective punishment. I grew up in an environment of silence following any punishment. I remember spankings as very traumatic and still can recall hurt feelings and anger about them. Mostly, I think I feel that way because I felt so unlovable because of my wrongs. I didn't understand mercy and grace.

One time when we visited my parents, I had spanked the two toddlers for some misdeed. Immediately afterward I held them on my lap and cried with them as we all recovered from the ordeal. My father walked by and scolded me severely for my error in undermining my punishment. My mind was in turmoil. I loved my father and hated to disagree with him, but every instinct told me I was doing the right thing. I gave that situation a lot of thought and prayer. I later determined to follow my own instincts. I continued to comfort my children following most episodes of punishment. I believe it minimized the periods of resentment and rebellion that sometimes accompany punishments.

The most important thing I convey to my children is that no deed could be so awful as to cause me to withhold my love and affection and acceptance from them. I think that knowledge allowed my children to overlook a great many of my other mistakes. It gave all of us room to offer each other lots of forgiveness and mercy.

As the children continue to grow, our responses to their moments of disobedience need to change. Punishment for grade-school-aged children and on into high school ages should fit the misdeed as closely as possible. It really should be more of a natural consequence from a poor decision rather than infliction of humiliation. Always remember to do everything you can to preserve the child's dignity and self-esteem. In some homes incidents of poor judgement become even greater incidents of belittling the already damaged psyche of a child.

Mark and Dad headed out in the family car for an early driving lesson. Big brother rode along in the back seat. Dad offered directions and somehow steered Mark down a quiet dead-end street with little or no room to turn around. While trying to crank the car around and shift gears and maneuver back and forth, the car ran over a turtle in the road. Already nervous and self-conscious, Mark immediately felt sick about what he had done.

All the way home Dad ridiculed his carelessness in smashing the turtle. He seemed unaware of the tears threatening to spill over in his humiliated son's throat and eyes. He acted more concerned about the dead turtle. The 16-year-old boy barely made it home and into his room. He didn't dare let his father or brother see him crying. His hasty exit only magnified the ridicule from the others.

Another form of humiliating treatment takes the form of name calling or negative labeling.

Suzy is preoccupied while washing the dishes and breaks the crystal salad bowl. Mom spouts, "You're so clumsy! Why can't you ever pay attention to what you're doing?" The mother's statement implies that Suzy never pays attention and always breaks things.

Name-calling and ridicule are not forms of discipline or punishment, but merely parents venting their emotions. Try hard to step back and hear yourself, so you can stop these behaviors before they become a pattern. Once they do become habits, it will probably take third-party intervention (professional counseling) to break the cycle.

Also be very careful of levying vengeful punishments simply because a child challenges your authority. To handle the situation when a child steps over the line of defiance is important, but letting things cool off before discussing consequences is also good. Threats made in anger from either parent or child can quickly get out of hand, and then stubborn pride makes us carry through on something we may later regret. Every child knows exactly what buttons to push to nudge his parent over the anger cliff. We parents are sometimes more predictable than our inventive children.

Take time frequently to experience and acknowledge the gentle mercies of God toward each of us whenever we disobey Him. His consequences are always natural and often mitigated. Let us use His example when we need to teach our children.

Teenagers will challenge their parents' authority, and it is wise to plan for that moment rather than reacting emotionally to it. It does affect our emotions. It hurts to have a defiant child. It hurts to have a child who is angry with us. But it will likely happen, so plan how you will respond. That will give you good protection from words or actions you might regret later.

A particularly challenging problem for many homes is teaching children to use a considerate tone of voice while playing and disagreeing with their siblings and parents. Occasionally the words will be correct, but the tone might be deadly. Included in this category of offense would also be the use of unacceptable words and phrases that all children like to try at some point in their life.

One solution for handling this thorny, persistent tongue issue could be "the onion." Any time bad or unkind words erupted, I peeled and sliced onion as dinner for the offending child. This provided an unusually graphic lesson to the entire family and not just the teary offender. (No one ever had to eat an entire onion, but they shouldn't know that when they sit down in front of it. After a child's good attempts to suffer the agony and accept the consequence, it's Ok for the parents to offer a little mercy.)

When a child cannot be ready for school on time morning after morning after morning, find something that fits the reason behind the lateness. Does the daughter take too long curling and recurling her hair? Then remove the curling iron for a week. Do the children have trouble getting out of bed? Then start the bedtime routine 30 minutes earlier each evening until they get up on time. Do they dawdle over finding the just-right shirt to wear today? Limit them to one choice every day for a week. Or make the choice the evening before, when you still have time to replace the missing button or do the ironing.

Further, start a chart and keep track of the days they arrive at the bus stop or into the car on time, and reward the behavior you want to continue. Make the children responsible for their own actions, and reward and acknowledge the good decisions they make.

Some children simply are not capable of hurrying, so be sure to give them extra preparation time with gentle nudges at regular intervals. Try to keep your own impatience and other negative feelings out of your voice, because they seem to slow down an already slow-paced child. On the other hand, when it's not necessary to hurry, allow the child the luxury of moving at his own natural pace. He doesn't have to rush into the house after school and change clothes in three minutes. He can dawdle over supper, though he has to watch the clock during breakfast. Try to be sensitive to the child's inborn pace. Some children grow up feeling labeled as lazy simply because they move more slowly than an efficient, energetic sibling.

Recently one of my children asked me why they were never grounded as teenagers, a punishment often mentioned by other teens. Well, punishment of children often means punishment for the parent also. And I disliked having to be grounded for a week in order to enforce the grounding of my children. In other words, do not levy a punishment that you will have difficulty enforcing. To expect a child of any age to enforce his own punishment is unrealistic.

Finding consequences that fit the wrong actions can be a difficult assignment and might require a bit more creativity than you feel. So be resourceful; meet with other parents and share ideas. Read books. Don't be limited as you journey through the land mined teen years. If you do attempt something that works effectively, share it with other parents. They will appreciate your hints.

Whatever approach you take to enforcing your code of required behavior, analyze it at regular intervals to be sure you are teaching and not just reacting. Always be aware of the dignity and honor you give to your children, even in the midst of a serious behavior flare-up. And remember to conduct yourself with control and with your own dignity intact. If you expect to be respected, you must act respectably.

Chapter 5

Obeying Creates Contentment

C hildren who respect their parents will obey them—at least most of the time. Parents who value their children will require and motivate their respect as well as their obedience. Obedience does not occur naturally, but it is the result of a determined commitment from parents to their children: a commitment first to help them have someone whom they trust enough to *want* to obey, and then someone to help them know *how* to obey.

This process begins soon after the arrival of a new baby from the hospital. As the baby grows into toddlerhood he also grows into the awareness that Mom and Dad can be trusted. They will feed him when he needs to eat. They will keep him warm and comfortable. They will hold him and love him. They will make funny faces, tickle, and evoke laughter. The little one learns he is loved and safe. When parents act like parents, the toddler will automatically begin the respect process.

However, some people do not expect to be respected. Some mothers assume that they are to play the role of servant or martyr to their children. They view the caretaking responsibilities as chores rather than an expression of love. Granted, it's hard to remember the reason we're washing dirty laundry while nursing a splitting headache, but we need to view all home tasks as part of our love for our family. When the chores, which are naturally mundane, cause us to lose our self-respect, we will no longer expect our children's respect. Maintaining self-respect and children's respect is a constant and conscious process.

Betsy and her three children often made our family welcome in their home. But I discovered something quite uncomfortable after several visits together. Whenever my children were present, they received all of Betsy's attention. She would scold her own children for the exact same behavior she complimented in my children. She provided food and snacks for my children and raved about their various accomplishments, while downplaying the achievements of her own children; though they were a very talented and intelligent group. She seemed to feel that my family was more important than her family—and that didn't feel right to me or to her children. She failed them and made them feel less loved and safe. Thus it was harder for them to want to obey her.

The overall attitude of loving and cherishing begins from the earliest days, and out of this comes the first step of earning our children's respect. Fortunately, child experts now advocate that you cannot spoil a child by holding and loving him too much. Take those words to heart and touch and love your children in any way you can. A doted-on baby is much easier to dote on as a preteen than one who is treated sternly from infancy. Changing the pattern is hard, so it is much easier to start as you intend to continue throughout your children's various stages. If lavishing affection on a baby is not bad, neither is it bad to lavish affection on a preteen or teenager. The young teen who may suddenly be more self-conscious of his body and of his ability to accept or extend affection still needs to receive it.

One of my children decided he was too old for hugs and kisses. I kept insisting I wasn't too old for hugs and kisses and invented the annoying "rule" that anyone who went to bed without giving Mom a hug and a kiss would get snuggled later in bed. Well, that was not a popular idea, so I usually received at least a grudging hug and sort of kiss on most nights. And after one incident of being snuggled later in their own bed (and I readily admit that I was not made welcome!) the bedtime routine of hugs and kisses was rarely skipped. And because we continued touching even through the awkward times, the reluctance lasted for a short time and was soon forgotten. Even now, as adults, my children—sons and daughters alike—will readily collapse onto my lap for a hug and snuggle. All of us need lots more hugs and touching than we receive in the ordinary course of life. Don't let your children go hungry for them (even if they act as if they don't care).

From the parent point of view, it's much easier to expect to be obeyed if we feel that we *deserve* to be obeyed. I hesitate to use the word *deserve*, but it's a fact of life that we like ourselves better when we do good things and treat others as they ought to be treated. Parents are no different than other people. If we behave in an appropriate manner, we can more readily expect our children to respect us and to behave in an appropriate manner. Do we conduct our lives in a way that exemplifies respectability?

Teaching our children to obey begins with loving them and then grows as we expect them to respect and obey us.

During the first three years of a child's life the foundation is laid upon which parents and their children will build the rest of their lives. The attitude of respect and the attitude of wanting to obey begins during those early months. Give your child simple requests, and then help him to follow your requests. For instance, try the approach of "let's do this together" rather than the "you do that." And keep the initial directions very simple. Remember the first approach of diverting a toddler about to attempt an action with which you don't agree.

The second way to handle an activity you don't want to happen (such as a pot of flowers about to be dumped) is to move yourself very quickly to the child's side and help him refrain from dumping the flowers rather than yelling across the room or out the window. Parenting from a recliner chair in front of the TV really doesn't work. Calling out directives to a playing child while you read the evening paper or wash the supper dishes rarely works either. The best way to create an environment of obedience is to physically assist the toddler in developing the behaviors that you feel are most important.

When your shouted or called requests are simple and infrequent, they are much more likely to be followed. A nagging mother usually becomes an ignored mother. A yelling father discovers at some point that no one is listening. Be aware of the manner in which you speak directives, and you might be surprised what you learn about yourself.

For many reasons prompt and strict obedience are important habits to develop within your children. One story I've told many times happened to childhood friends of mine.

The family hiked often on Sabbath afternoons and were hiking this particular Sabbath with two other families. Suddenly the quiet play of the children was disrupted by a called command from the father. "Stan, stop! Don't take another step." Stan did as he was asked and turned back to face his father. One more step would have landed his foot directly atop a rattlesnake. Practiced obedience saved his life that day. And the key word in this sentence is "practiced." Begin immediately teaching and expecting your baby and your toddler to obey you. Make it easy and rewarding for them to do so.

An important step in making it easy for the children to obey involves the parent's decision to recognize the children's playtime as valuable. We need to avoid interruptive requests and thoughtless demands while our children are in the midst of play. It will be more natural for our children to respect us if we respect them and the activities that engage their attention.

A mother I knew a long time ago dealt with bouts of illness that confined her to bed and couch. Movement was sometimes difficult and always painful, so whenever she needed something, she called out to her children to fetch and wait on her. Her frequent interruptions of their play created too many resentments and tensions. She became impatient with their disobedience and lack of respect, while the children became angry and disgusted with Mom's illness. Had the mother been able to recognize the wisdom of timing her requests to breaks between games, much of the frustration on both sides could have been avoided. Remembering to make it easy for our children to want to obey takes lots of insight.

At the beginning of this chapter I used the word *commitment* from parents to teach the children to obey. Teaching children is not easy—and it's a task never finished. To choose what you want your children to value and then consistently to lay your values in front of them is important.

For example, Dad tells Mom that he will do the dishes and clean up the kitchen after dinner tonight. But by the time the meal is over he's tired, so he stretches out on the couch in front of the TV for a while. Then he remembers something else he has to do and before he knows it, he's tired and off to bed. Meanwhile, the dinner dishes sit drying and dirty, still on the table. The next morning at breakfast, those same unwashed dishes sit in testimony of a promise broken. Hmm. Is Dad's word still good? Will he do the other things he's said he'll do?

On the way to school Mom drives several miles over the speed limit and cuts off other drivers as she quickly changes lanes without warning. Later she scolds Sonny for disobeying the teacher. Hasn't she given an example of disobedience and thinking of herself first?

I could share dozens more ugly examples from my own life: examples I have had to examine and to admit did not show my children what I would choose for them to do; examples of behaviors I needed to change in order to be a parent worthy of being respected and obeyed.

A difficult part of teaching children is the frequent (or constant) interruptions. Parents rarely get the luxury of a completed conversation—whether on the phone or in person. Children demand attention and will do most anything to achieve it. If you and your children are in the same house, expect to be interrupted and decide what you will do about it. Will you ignore all obnoxious behavior while you visit with friends? Or will you quietly excuse yourself and hold your child accountable for discourtesy or whatever stunt they have pulled and then return to your friend? (Remember Chapter 2, when we discussed protecting your child's dignity in front of others.) Will you put the phone call on hold and restrain the soccer ball from sailing across the table?

Another side of this issue concerns teaching children to acknowledge and to be courteous to your adult friends. Have you ever been visiting with someone when you couldn't complete a sentence without being interrupted either by the child or by the parent constantly attending the child? A child can be taught to wait and to play quietly while a parent has a bit of grown-up conversation. Unruly children can alienate friendships. So while we don't want to neglect our children, we can develop a balance in how we allocate our attention.

The commitment part of teaching children to obey comes from staying on duty at all times in all circumstances. And the amazing thing is that your child will give you frequent tests to find which events cause you to go off duty. They want to know if you are a full-time parent or a part-time parent. And they choose a full-time parent. It does matter to them.

Another hard part about the parenting-respect issue is the times a mom or a dad decides he and the children should be best friends. Companionship between parents and their growing up children is a precious and delightful experience. However, when the companionship supersedes the parental authority, the child loses something important. Whenever a parent brags about her and her teenaged daughter being best friends or more like sisters than mother and daughter, it means the child does not have a parent. And a child that age without a parent is in real danger. Children vacillate between adulthood and childhood many times before they actually become adults. In the meantime, to know that an adult is on duty is important.

When choosing to be our child's friend rather than their parent, we are abdicating a lot of our responsibilities on that child's behalf. We begin making decisions based on popularity rather than for the child's best long-term good. Sometimes we moms and dads have to make tough decisions that make our sons and daughters quite angry with us for a time and we have to be willing to let them be angry with us. We have to show them that our unconditional love can survive their anger. We have to prove our love to them again and again, because they won't feel very lovable for a wide variety of teenaged reasons. When we become their friend, we let a lot of our respect slip away, and then it's much harder for a child to continue to obey. Once the cycle is broken, it's very hard to reclaim the role of parent.

Another pitfall I discovered en route to successful parenting (a standard toward which I still strive!) came from my unlimited list of expectations for my four children. I issued more rules and lists than even I could remember, so, of course, my children couldn't begin to remember them all. That left me constantly nagging after some minor forgotten rule, and consequently I missed the big issues because I ran out of energy. Perfect obedience to all my wishes became impossible. It took me only 10 or 11 years to realize what a monster I had created. And I felt overwhelmed. My children were out of control, and so was I.

I learned that no matter the age of the children, the list of rules needs to be short and simple. Over time, we hoped some of the desired behaviors would become habit and not topics of obedience. But in the meantime I learned to make many fewer requests and to insist that those few requests be promptly and exactly followed. All of us felt better. I was less overwhelmed with things to remember, and the children knew exactly what to expect from themselves and from me.

I reviewed the list of my expectations and chose the three most important things for my children to learn. I began to pare my requirements down into something much more manageable for them as well as for me. If a parent requires strict obedience, the expectations must be simply and carefully defined. And enforcing a few well-stated rules is much easier than always being after a hundred nebulous ones.

So from painful experience I suggest that if you find your children suffering from a spate of total disregard for parental authority, first take a good serious look at your own role. Are you demanding and disrespectful toward your children's feelings and activities? Are you inconsistent? Are you overloading them (and yourself)? It never hurts to get a second opinion from someone who knows you and your family well. Ask your parents, your friends, possibly your mate (if you're not too defensive to accept his or her comments), a teacher, or other professional who might interact with you and your children for suggestions to improve your children's obedience quotient.

Parents who believe they already know everything simply because they are parents quickly become a detriment to themselves as well as to their children. Parenting is a learning, growing, changing, and experimental process. No sooner will you think you know exactly how to handle something than your next child comes along with a whole new set of personality traits and reactions. Be open to suggestions for personal improvement, because it can be multiplied in the lives of your mate and in the lives of your children. Every personal-growth step you make becomes a ripple in the bigger pond of the whole family. This is really worth the effort in the case of long-term effects.

Probably the most important single thing we do for ourselves, for our children, and in tribute to our heavenly Father involves our continual decision to honor and obey God. The example of Mom and Dad choosing to obey God, choosing to *want* to obey God even when it doesn't always come easily or even make sense, will illustrate how we expect our children to obey us and then, in turn, to obey God. By our own obedience and then by our encouragement of our children's obedience, we give them the opportunity to live in harmony with heaven.

One family whom I knew years ago lived as nearly to "perfect" as they were able to. They ate correctly and lived temperately in almost every area of their life. They followed as many of the prescribed "rules" of Christian lifestyle as anyone I have known. But they didn't enjoy the life they felt consigned to live. They lived this life without the love and enjoyment of God's company. They obeyed God without affection but in a spirit of duty. Consequently they gave their children a negative picture of God and of obedience to Him. The children grew to resent and disrespect their parents as they saw through the charade of their lives.

So when we choose to live a Christian lifestyle and offer that inheritance to our children, we need to be sure that our hearts and our actions are in harmony. Obedience without the joy of God's companionship is sterile and unrewarding. We can show our children how to combine those attributes and give them a much fuller life in our homes now and for all eternity.

Chapter 6

Modeling Mercy

By the time your child starts school, he should have learned that you are safe to trust and your love for each other will be so highly developed that obedience will come quite naturally. However, if you expect that you will have any perfectly behaved children, you are certainly set up for disappointment.

So another important tool we need to give our children is the example of what to do when we make mistakes. Yes, I said *example*. And this is another one of those really hard parts of being a parent, because it is not a popular concept for parents to admit to their children when they err. Mostly we parents are expected to model proper and perfect behavior to our children, and that under the guise of respect and authority we are never to be challenged about our actions.

This idea sets our children up to be dishonest and defensive about their own mistakes. If we cannot admit when we are wrong, what right do we have to expect our children to admit they are wrong?

I must confess that this is not something I understood or recognized for the first many years of being a parent. I discovered I was raising children who could not admit when they made mistakes because I never acknowledged my own mistakes. One of my children became an accomplished truth evader, another became adept at rationalization. Another became sneaky. And all of us made many mistakes in our treatment of one another in the course of our daily lives.

Since my job and the accompanying commute caused me to arrive home a couple hours after my children came home from school, I instituted certain chore requirements in order to support the lifestyle of our active household. Consequently, when I arrived home from work, I held specific expectations about what I would see within my home. I created lists and talked often on the phone, so my expectations were quite clearly defined.

I knew my tendency to shout, yell, and carry on when I entered a cluttered, disorganized house. I also had little patience for children at play when an unfinished job list was still on the counter or homework was undone. I always advised that work comes before play. So on my drive home I would determine to be patient with my children's probable shortcomings and commit to refrain from an unpleasant tirade. Somehow that seemed to be a futile attempt, because if I opened the door to chaos, my tone and words immediately added to the confusion.

One evening at worship (which followed the supper hour in our home) I felt I could not pray with my children until I confessed my wrong behavior. Previously I had justified my outbursts by my children's failures to do what they should have done. It was actually *their* fault that I yelled and lost control. (Oh, the games we play with our minds to rationalize our shortcomings.) They *owed* me a neat and orderly household upon my arrival home since I worked so hard to provide this home for them. I don't know that I actually defined those exact excuses, but I felt them.

I resisted the urge to apologize to my children that evening, and the next day I sought advice from a couple of wise friends who were experienced and successful Christian parents. The first friend I spoke with quickly defended my outbursts. Of course I had a right to expect the chores to be finished when I arrived home. I didn't hurt the children any if I only yelled and didn't actually hit them. Somehow those words only reinforced my own sense of guilt and wrongness. Yelling and screaming did not seem to be appropriate parental behavior.

The second friend appeared horrified at the thought that a parent would apologize and admit weakness to a child. He was sure the children would never be able to respect or obey me in the future if I allowed them to see me as capable of a mistake. He insisted, "Parents do not apologize to children." But, he added, it probably wouldn't hurt if I tried harder to keep my temper under control when I came home from work.

Somehow this counsel didn't feel right to me either. At lunchtime I took a long walk and tried to pray and seek heavenly counsel. My prayers didn't feel right either. I'm not sure I was a good listener, with so much confusion in my heart and head. On the drive home I continued to ask God's wisdom on this issue.

Later the same evening I again joined the children in evening worship. Before we began our worship activity, one of the children piped up with a story about her brother's misbehavior at school that day. He had treated a friend badly, and she was concerned the friendship might be damaged. When I looked at the offending son, he hung his head and admitted he had done wrong but quickly and sincerely added that he hadn't meant to hurt anyone. Now what could he do?

Without a second of silence, I suggested he could go to the phone right now and call his friend and tell him he was sorry. The friendship was far too valuable to let pride stand between the two boys. We waited worship while my son made his phone call, and all of a sudden I realized I had just given myself the answer I had been seeking all day. My children were far more important than the false pride of pretending to be a perfect parent.

As I poured out my heart and regrets and apologies to my children they quickly offered hugs and forgiveness, and with teary voices promised to try harder to have the house ready for my arrival home each day. Our hearts united in prayer and love for a special hour of worship and praise to God.

Had I refused to submit my pride to give that most important apology, I would have erected a barrier of stubbornness between my children and me. My shame and discomfort would probably have become more pronounced and my tolerance would undoubtedly have grown even more sensitive. The children would have become more defensive and protective of their positions in what might have become a family war. Family worship would certainly have become a hundredfold less meaningful and personal as our level of sharing became sterile and surface.

But by humbling myself in genuine sorrow for my actions and words, I opened the door for honesty and acceptance. I bared my heart, and the children responded by opening their own hearts. Further, I modeled the way I hoped my children would later react when they knew they, too, had wronged someone else.

Friends of our family went through a traumatic situation a few years ago. The father, who worked as an office manager of a very large firm, one day used business money for a personal purpose. Stu worked in a position of significant respect and responsibility and led out in the children's ministry of the church where his entire family attended. He had changed many lives with the touch of Jesus. The theft of those dollars was a definite aberration of behavior. But that did not allow for any mercy or concealment when upper management discovered his misdeed. Instantly he lost his job and found his name in the local newspapers. He must pay serious penalties.

I visited their home, hastily relocated to obtain privacy, and talked with his wife. She found herself looking for a job after years out of the market and wondered how her three daughters would ever handle this. The girls were in the upper grades and in junior high. Of course the sudden move upset their routine, and they were going to have to transfer schools. The father's mistake and the ensuing consequences affected everyone in the family.

As Janey and I talked I asked how Stu was handling things with the family. She commented that she was actually quite proud of him. He accepted full responsibility for his actions and apologized with anguish. He had been very thankful for their companionship and for the children's pledges of support for him. He also had sought out a counselor and seemed committed to paying whatever price had to be paid and making the necessary changes to right the wrong. And then she stated again that she wondered what this would do to the children.

Remembering my interaction with my own children only a few days previous, I suggested to Janey that perhaps he had given them a very good example of how to behave. She seemed puzzled. I told her my own story. Though my actions had not had quite the same level of repercussions, I still had admitted my sins to God, to myself, and then to my children. That confession created unity and allowed my children to offer me forgiveness and help to prevent me continuing to sin in the same manner.

Janey said instantly, "Oh, I know Stu will never ever be tempted to take something again." I smiled and assured her that I believed her. She agreed that the children believed him too. I reminded her that we all sin at times, and the important part of the process was even more about how we reacted after we did wrong than the wrong itself. A sin committed once and truly repented of is a far different situation than a continuous repetition of the same sin without repentance and confession.

Somehow I've come to realize that confession really does preclude continuous repetition of the same sin. I hate to admit in a public forum how many years I had let myself get away with yelling or screaming in frustration at my children. Fortunately, it hadn't kept them from loving me, but how much our relationship grew once I confessed my shame at such nasty behavior! And, additionally, I found it much easier to discontinue the unlovely words and tones once I had confessed them aloud to my children.

I am sorry my friends had to go through such a traumatic and shameful experience. But I do not believe their adult and honest handling of it caused any long-lasting harm to their children. Quite the opposite in fact. I think those three girls have received an excellent example of how to handle the transgressions in their own lives.

Honestly admit to yourself that you did indeed do wrong. Accept blame for your own actions, rather than to place it artificially on someone or something else. Then kneel before God and seek His promised forgiveness and cleansing.

I have also discovered that it's hard to repent for something if we don't admit we've done wrong. But once I've admitted I did do something wrong, I can't get onto my knees fast enough. The weight of unconfessed sin is far too great for me to carry. And as I stay on my knees I try to visualize God's cleansing process and watch His spirit washing my soiled heart, making it white and pure again.

That process allows me to accept God's forgiveness and enables me to swallow stubborn pride and continue to the next step, which is to confess and apologize to the one or ones I have wronged (very often the people I love are the ones I hurt). We might not always be forgiven by these people as readily as my four children forgave me that one night (and several other times since then), but we still must seek their forgiveness and then allow them however much time they need to respond.

And then comes the natural part of the process, restitution. For my friend Stu, this meant repaying the dollars he took as well as paying the price to society for breaking the law. His humble acceptance of this punishment enhanced his stature in his family and in the wider community of his church.

This enhanced stature and continued respect from my children surprised me at first in my own experience until I started watching people around me and analyzing the attitudes of the people I respected the most in my little world. It's far easier to respect a person who is honest with himself as well as with others. Trust is a part of respect, and confession creates an atmosphere of trust.

My friends gave me bad counsel, but they did teach me that the only source for true wisdom comes from heaven—and that heaven often uses our children to teach us the important lessons we parents must learn.

And now that the lesson is learned, we must allow ourselves to apply it to our children. Each one of my children has made at least one, if not several, serious mistakes—mistakes with shameful consequences and lots of personal trauma. Each time this has happened, I have been sure that my heart would burst with pain, and I have been absolutely at a loss as to what my role was in the incident.

A couple years ago in the Seattle area an arsonist lurked in alleys and caused serious damage in several neighborhoods. The police were baffled as they investigated and explored the scenes, looking for clues. One family began to recognize the clues as possibly belonging to their troubled son. So they did their own research and confirmed their worst fears. They met with their son and showed him what they had found, then went together with their son to meet with an attorney and confess to the police. Reporters swarmed the grieving parents and begged for an explanation. Why would parents turn their own son into the police?

Despite their pain, the parents explained that they could not protect and condone their son's actions, but he was their son; they loved him and would stand with him, offering him their constant love, support, and forgiveness. Additionally they offered apologies and made personal visits to each of the persons victimized in the son's crimes. But the son never appeared in court without both parents at his side.

One time when one of my children faced a serious incident at school I asked the dean what my role should be. My heart was broken, and I alternately wanted to strangle the child or hide him in my arms. The wise dean advised that my job was to love, listen, and forgive. Stand beside my son with arms opened wide—and to pray a lot. I followed his advice as best I could.

A couple days ago I asked my son how he was able to cope and grow so much from that time. He quickly responded, "Haven't I ever told you? It was you. Your forgiveness let me believe that God really could forgive me too." Wow!

Chapter 7

Decision Dilemma

C ourtney whipped the car around the corner and
tried unsuccessfully to make a U-turn at the next
intersection. She had passed the service station. Becky pretended to stay
calm in the passenger seat. A few moments later they were stopped beside
the correct gas pump, and Becky offered to pump the gas while Courtney
went inside to pay. Then Becky discovered the gas tank opening on the
opposite side from the pumps and hoses. She tugged and pulled, trying to
stretch the hoses to the opening. Meanwhile Courtney stood at the counter
unsure whether to pay cash or use her parents' gas card.

Becky couldn't wait to get back home. The entire day had been far more
stressful than she could have imagined. Courtney acted like a colt out of the
pasture for the first time as the two 18-year-old girls drove from Seattle to
Spokane for the day. The drive was long and the business tedious, but they
had managed to squeeze in a bit of fun. The two of them usually shared lots
of laughs and talked nonstop. They loved to listen and sing along with the
radio or their cassettes. But now it was late. They were both wearing down,
it was dark, and they still had miles to go before they got home.

And everything that could go wrong, had gone wrong. Courtney left her wallet at the first gas station, once she had been able to decide which station to use. Then they got lost. She had left the directions at home and Courtney didn't want to call and admit she'd forgotten them. But despite the mess-ups, Courtney kept telling Becky how grown up she felt to be in charge of her first trip. Secretly Becky kept thinking how ungrown-up she acted.

The next day Courtney called Becky at home and told her she'd been grounded. Her parents were furious with her mistakes and informed her that she couldn't be trusted to do anything right. No more all-day excursions unless her mother went along. Becky dropped the phone with a sigh. She loved to do things with Courtney, but Courtney's parents complicated every little thing. Maybe if they'd let her do something on her own once in a while, she would learn how to handle things and not get so scatterbrained.

I think Becky is absolutely right. However, the scariest thing we parents ever do is to let our children make their own decisions. After all, we have many more years of experience and can prevent much difficulty by making their decisions for them. Furthermore, what if a teenager makes the wrong decision? Think of all the protection we can provide for our children by keeping them in the cocoon of our own homes.

Freedom to let children make their own decisions is especially difficult for a parent with strong religious convictions. Suppose a child errs and commits a sin by choosing wrong? It might be a lot worse than making a wrong turn or fumbling with choosing a gas station. Many parents fear so much for their children's spiritual safety that they create an artificial world for them to live in.

I delve into this topic with fear and trembling, yet I believe strongly that children must be allowed to make age-appropriate decisions, even if the decisions are wrong and have unpleasant consequences. The key words here are "age-appropriate" decisions.

Two-year-old Patti loved to choose her own clothes. Of course she had no idea what the day would hold when she dressed in the morning, but her opinions were definite. Consequently the mother and daughter had frequent power struggles over what Patti would wear each day until one day Mother realized how foolish these disagreements were. So each evening before bedtime, Mother started offering three choices (or less if it was close to laundry day!) of acceptable clothes for the next day's wear. Patti made her choice between these suggestions and felt content. She had been allowed to choose for herself.

Similarly, in the wintertime mother let her choose whether she wanted the pink mittens or the red ones. It didn't really matter if the mittens matched her coat.

If you decide to allow a young child to choose which pajamas to wear, you might want to make it an occasional choice. Also, if the little one decides to make the choice process a stalling tactic for facing bedtime, set a time in which the selection must be made or else make it yourself. For instance, if he has not chosen which pajamas to wear and does not have them on by 7:30, Dad will choose for him. Beware of letting decisions become a power struggle or manipulative issue. Keep things natural and matter-of-fact.

At bedtime we liked to read books with a spiritual theme rather than some of the more playful stories from the bookshelf. So I would make two or more selections of the type of story I wanted for this story time and then let the children take turns choosing which story we would read.

At the dinner table we should allow the child to make some choices also. Friends of ours permitted each child one food he would *not* have to eat. At some meals one food could be skipped on the child's plate whenever it was served.

These seem like small choices, but they allow each child the opportunity to practice making decisions—safe decisions with no right or wrong consequences. Children who are given the freedom to make some of their own decisions have a much better sense of self-confidence and assurance. They also feel smart and important.

When children make some of their own life decisions they can accept more easily that some decisions must come from the parents. When the parents make all of the little as well as the big decisions, the child finds it more necessary to go through a time of rebellion. And sometimes rebellion begins very young.

Suzy decided that she did not want to attend school. She didn't like her teacher. The main reason she didn't like the teacher is because she was different than her first grade teacher had been. So Suzy did not go to school. The school year was into the second week before Suzy's mother decided she had to attend whether she wanted to or not.

Suzy's decision *not* to attend school is a good example of an inappropriate decision for a second-grader to make. She should have had absolutely no choice about whether or not to attend school.

My friend Cathy made that choice for her daughters, even though it wasn't easy. Cathy has very shy daughters, and they were new to the school. The girls were ready to enter second and fifth grades. They refused to enter the classrooms and ran to hide in the bathrooms. Their mother visited the teachers, confiding the difficulty and reporting to them the location of the girls. Then she left, and the teachers and other students quickly absorbed the girls into the classroom situations.

Other age-appropriate decisions might be whether to take piano lessons or not. I believed that piano lessons were as important as reading, writing, and arithmetic, so the decision to take or not to take did not rest with the children. However, the decision of whether to practice in the morning before school or after school before play did belong to the children. Once they decided when to practice, they had to practice at the same time each day and couldn't be constantly vacillating. So they began to learn the consequences of making certain decisions.

Many children allowed to make the decision to quit piano lessons after only one month or one year later regret their inability to play the piano or read music. Thus, I recommend that parents make piano lesson decisions for most grade school children. Work together and make the child feel a part of the decision, but find ways to motivate and encourage so that the lessons will be a successful experience. If, after a fair period of time, you discover your child really does not have piano potential, you might find an alternate activity.

Respect in the Family

In our home one of the children practiced faithfully but simply did not progress. Meanwhile the siblings learned quickly and easily. His practice sessions were agonizing, and he worked very hard without results. By the fifth-grade year he began playing the trombone, so I felt it might be a good time to let the trombone replace the piano. Rarely had he complained or asked to be excused from the piano, because he understood it was a family requirement, but the relief he manifested when I made the suggestion he could consider changing instruments was dramatic.

On the other side, one of the children showed great ability and propensity for excellence on the piano but grew tired of the routine. I made the challenge that she could cease taking lessons when she had mastered every hymn in the church hymnal. By the time she achieved that goal, she no longer talked about quitting. Today she is a professional musician and feels grateful to have been encouraged to continue taking lessons.

So we do need to be sensitive about making arbitrary decisions, and we should plan to include the children in some decisions concerning their activities. But we are still the parents, and it's alright to encourage younger children to make the decisions we feel are best.

The grade school years are important in preparing children to begin making more of their own decisions. And the more decisions they are allowed to make, the more their confidence will increase and the better opinion they will have of themselves. Beware of falling into the trap of acting as if the children are permitted to make a decision and then lecturing them thoroughly about all the reasons they should make the decision you want them to make. Then avoid pouring on guilt if they choose other than you think they should have chosen. Definitely don't say "I told you so" when they make a decision you didn't want them to make and it goes wrong. Remember that the child already feels foolish and stupid. Give children time to digest their pride, and discuss the situation after emotions have subsided.

During this time of practice decisions, use every opportunity to teach the values you want your children to emulate. Teenagers do not decide to avoid drugs while the pills rest in their friend's outstretched hands. They do not decide *not* to drink alcohol while riding in a car full of friends already drinking. And they certainly don't decide not to become sexually active while sitting in a convertible overlooking the city on a moonlit night. All these decisions and many more are made long before the opportunity arises. Our job as parents is to equip them to make the right decision before they are faced with it and then to practice how they will handle those difficult, peer pressured moments.

The decision to attend college is not made during the senior year of high school. Begin talking about it and planning aloud for it from the time your children are in grade school. Engage your children in dreaming, planning, and making their own goals from a young age. Get them in the habit of goal setting and thinking toward their future.

Recently I read a newspaper account about a 17-year-old young man who won a new car and decided to sell it back to the dealership and save the money for college or offer it to his parents for paying bills. He made this decision without input from his parents. Somewhere along his journey he had practiced and learned the art of making decisions for his own long-term good. I found myself wondering what decision my 17-year-olds would have made and wondering if I had prepared them to make such a decision.

"Being confident of this very thing, that He who has begun a good work in you will complete it until the day of Jesus Christ." (Phil. 1:6, NKJV). Do we believe this verse? Then we will trust God to bring our children into a saved relationship with Him.

My children have made far too many wrong decisions. I will spare them the embarrassment of recounting those errors here in print, but I have to say that their mistakes caused me serious agony. Sometimes I would have liked to scream, lecture, and strangle. I did spout and pace and ramble on, but rarely in the presence of the one who had done wrong. I am an emotional person and without the companionship of a husband I probably expressed my emotions too often in the presence of the other children. But I did act out my constant love for the offending child and express words and actions of forgiveness, even when my heart hadn't caught up with those words yet.

Sometimes our children's wrong decision will have long-term consequences that will be hard for them and for us to bear. But that's the price of parenting. We will walk the path of consequences with our children rather than trying to bail them out. It may mean swallowing a lot of pride and learning to live with embarrassment, but the companionship of your restored child is far more valuable than a little bit of pride.

In the '70s a pastor family I knew had a son who wore the long hair of the era and listened to disreputable music. The parents were so embarrassed and anxious about their son's sins that they made those behaviors far more important than the love and companionship they could have offered. This family continues to be estranged and devoid of mutual respect.

Somehow we have to learn how to supersede the judgments of other people. We need to make our children feel loved and valuable, even when they live a different life than the one we have chosen for ourselves.

When teenagers learn how to become adults, they will do a lot of going back and forth as they experiment with lifestyles and activities, learning which things they want to claim. And some days they will seem quite grown up, while on other days you won't be able to recall the grown-up moments. Be patient and try to hold your tongue as often as possible.

My rules mostly covered intervention only during times of destruction—when the children were making bad decisions that were hurting themselves or other people. Some things are mostly just unwise, but other decisions cause damage, and that would be a time to intervene. Many books have been written on tough-love concepts, and extreme behaviors will necessitate extreme actions by the parent.

By the time our children attain the level of college students, we really need to encourage them to be adults. As much as possible they need to make most of their own decisions and be accountable for the results of those decisions. They need to know that they and God alone can face and endure any experience. And they won't learn that lesson if Mom and Dad come to the rescue in every unpleasant situation. Our children then will respect us a whole lot more than they would if we interfered and judged all of their daily decisions.

When we offer them the freedom to make mistakes, we minimize the amount of rebellion they will have to express in order to figure out who they are and who they want to be. They can practice making decisions in the safety of their parents' home, or they will escape and make even more drastic decisions without parental support.

We will attain this level of letting go on behalf of our children only if we have already learned the habit of praying constantly for our children in every circumstance. Each night before I sleep I verbally and visually tuck my children into the arms of Jesus. I picture Him in a giant rocking chair, holding each of my children close to His breast as they sleep. This gives me the peace in my heart that I need in order to be the mother they want me to be. When we truly trust God to love our children, we can trust Him also to protect them even in their foolishness and inexperience.

Each child will arrive at the destination of adulthood in a different way and at a different time. Our job as parents is to equip them with experience and confidence and a trust in God and in themselves. When they feel respected and look to their parents with respect, having a discussion and seeking advice willingly from their parents when a difficult decision looms will be much easier. And there will be plenty of difficult decisions. We make it much easier for our children if we have cultivated the environment of mutual respect and a place where interactive conversation can comfortably precede important decisions.

Let's go back to Courtney. Her parents made many of the ordinary decisions of her everyday life because they loved her and wanted to spare her the discomfort of a wrong decision. Additionally, they felt a determined sense of preserving their community image as a perfect family. They also wanted to protect Courtney from the harsh realities of life and the tendency of young people to make irreversible wrong decisions. But in being protected so firmly, she had no experience in making decisions and she suffered low self-esteem because she knew she made stupid decisions when she did have the opportunity to make them.

In the previous chapter we talked about learning how to react when we make mistakes. I suggest that the more we understand and experience

God's accepting forgiveness for our mistakes as parents, the more we will entrust our children to that same loving God.

I can remember falling on my knees some nights when the children were still quite young and feeling completely overwhelmed with the responsibility of raising my children to know and love Jesus. I felt inadequate. I wept and prayed, and somehow I came to understand that no matter how much I loved my children, God loved them more. It became clear to me that my job was to commit them to God and point them to Him.

The times I attempted to make all their decisions and protect them from their own immaturity were the times I trusted and walked with God the least. Controlling parents begin to act like God in their children's lives, and in my own case that became a violation of the first commandment. I had to love God and my children enough to let them go and let them fumble in the safe hands of their much wiser and much stronger heavenly Father.

Chapter 8

Learning to Listen

"Mommy! Mommy! Guess what happened today."
Eight-year-old Susie ran into the house—mouth first. Her exuberance halted midstream as she entered the family room and saw Mom on the phone with her fingers on her lips indicating silence. "Later," she silently framed the word.

Susie turned away in dejection. After putting her schoolbag away and changing her clothes, she came back to tell her tale. Busily mixing and measuring in the kitchen, Mommy was still too distracted to listen to Susie. "After dinner," she promised the disappointed girl.

Finally "after dinner" arrived, and Susie was actively playing with her brother, so Mom didn't interrupt the happy play. At bedtime she asked Susie what she had wanted to tell her earlier, and Susie just shrugged, "Oh, nothing."

The next day Mom met Susie's teacher at the grocery store. The teacher bubbled about Susie's adventure at school the day before and concluded with "I'm sure you're as proud of Susie as I am." Mom smiled and tried to give an appropriate response as she made a speedy escape. Whatever Susie had wanted to tell her last night must have been pretty important.

Listening to our children might be the best gift we can give to them. We cannot know when our children have something important to say, but we can know that our children are always important. And that's the difference between a parent who listens and one who doesn't.

Good listening has many components. One time I needed to peek inside one of my children's minds and learn why things were happening as they were. So I decided to take him to dinner alone—a rare event in our household. We had a pleasant meal and excellent visit, but on the way home he asked me why I didn't like him. After a high quality evening and such good communication, I certainly had not expected this horrible question. Stumped, I asked, "What on earth do you mean by that?"

"Well, the whole time we were talking, you were straightening my collar, brushing my hair back and harping about my dirty fingernails. It made me feel like you didn't like me."

Amazing how I could feel good about the same hour my son felt badly about. But I learned an important lesson. Listening to my children means accepting them exactly as they are: tousled hair, wrinkled shirt, and all. I took my son to dinner alone because I wanted him to feel special and separate, not just one of "the children." Instead I had zeroed in on him and subconsciously spent the whole time adjusting him to appear acceptable to me. I thought we had been talking, sharing, and really communicating. But all those efforts were for naught because, by my little actions, he felt unliked.

I recall a speaker at workers' meeting talking to the pastors' wives about relationships with their teenagers. She had said, "If your child comes into the kitchen to talk to you while you're drying dishes, turn around so quickly to look at him that you drop a dish. If it breaks, so what? Show your child by your physical responses that he is more important than an old dish." I remember the woman sitting next to me wondering, Whatever did she mean? What did breaking dishes have to do with listening to your children? I think I just now began to understand her point. I had made clean fingernails more important than my child. I guess I needed to drop a plate on the kitchen floor.

In the following paragraphs I am going to share some of the things I have learned about listening to my children. The art of good parental listening is a continually developing skill and a key ingredient to maintaining your child's sense of self-worth and esteem. The most important compliment you will pay any person is the gift of giving his words and thoughts the value of your time and attention.

Good listening cannot be a scheduled activity. Children are moody and impulsive creatures (somewhat like their parents), and when the words burst out of their mouths, that's precisely the moment you need to give them your attention. Two hours later the enthusiasm and intensity will be greatly diminished, and you will have missed out on the heart of their story.

In our house the times most likely to hear the best stories are the moments immediately after arrival home—the closer to the end of the school day, the richer the story. Immediately after the ball game, the more thrilling the account of the double play. Several hours or a day later, the account would probably be, "Oh, yeah, I made a double play at the game." End of story.

The second most likely time to listen to my children's hearts is after the house is quiet at the end of the day. The telephone doesn't ring then. The TV is turned off. The other children are tucked into bed in their own rooms. At that time the child thinks, *Now I have Mom's full attention without distraction. And no one else will hear.* I know lots of parents who are very rigid about bedtimes, for themselves as well as for their children. I had to learn to be flexible. I had to learn to trust God to restore my energy without the hours in bed I knew I ordinarily needed.

My being a single parent, made it easier for my children to plan on alone time with me, or me with them, but couples can create opportunities for children to talk with them separately. Rarely will a child open his heart to two people at once. Talking with only one parent is less threatening. Sometimes children will feel closer to one parent than to the other. This is very normal, and I urge all parents to avoid letting hurt feelings or jealousy damage this closeness. Often at different ages a child will choose a different confidant.

An exception to talking with one parent at a time would be the friend I knew who used to go into her parents' room, sit on their bed in the dark, and talk comfortably about almost any topic. Darkness gives a sense of privacy and intimacy.

One time that I remember quite clearly occurred while my children were in high school. My youngest son was in the midst of a very complicated situation and decided to talk it through late one night. The details were tangled, complex, and emotional. He had a lot of sorting out to do. I listened. I asked questions. As I listened I yawned but refused to look at the clock. By the end of our talk, he had reached some decisions and figured out how to handle some of the issues. Additionally, we felt very close to each other because we had shared an emotional and deep experience. We prayed together, and my son went to bed feeling loved and confident that he had a wise mother. (I knew I wasn't, but my attention gave him the impression I was.) He also had the courage to follow through on the things he knew he should do, because he knew he wasn't alone. And he knew I would be praying for him.

I went to bed at 3:00 a.m. that night and faced a full day of work the next day. I gave my fatigue to Jesus and fell instantly asleep. Early the next morning I awakened to my oldest son tugging on my shoulder. "Mom, can we talk a little before you go to work today?" I climbed out of my unconscious cave and determined to wake up enough to listen.

Another problem lay before me as this son unburdened his heart and struggled to make sense of a confusing situation. Again, I mostly listened and asked a few questions. Together we came up with a workable solution. We hugged, we prayed, and my son went off to school with the confidence he needed.

That night at worship both boys shared the conclusions of their stories. Both had found clarity and peace where before they had been muddled and confused. All I had really offered them was my heart and my time, and together we had looked to Jesus for wisdom. And what a united team we were that night as we rejoiced!

Yes, I had been tired during the day, but the exhilaration of sharing my children's love and respect was far more valuable than a few more hours in bed could ever have been. And I learned again how important it was for me to be a praying mother. My prayers for my children did make a difference.

Another thing I learned over a long period of time is that talking to someone who genuinely listens to you allows you to make your own decisions much more intelligently. Lots of us (not just the Wolcott clan) think out loud and discover how to decide and handle situations by talking them through. In the previous chapter we talked about helping our children make wise decisions. One of the most important ways we can do that is by listening attentively to them as they think aloud. By the time all their thoughts and feelings are aired, they usually have reached a sensible conclusion.

Sometimes the things our children want to talk about won't seem very important to us as adults, but we need to practice active listening and respectful attitudes regardless of the topic. We will be able to give the subject matter the right attention only because we have chosen to value and respect the person sharing the information.

Physically active people who are driven to be involved in productive pursuits at all times sometimes falter in their ability to be good listeners to their children. First, I encourage you to be such an actively involved listener while your child talks that you will forget your body isn't busy. Second, look for ways to listen actively at the same time you're completing a task. For example, talk together while washing and drying dishes. I would guess more hearts have been cleansed at the kitchen sink than have dishes. Another time to have good heart-to-heart conversation is while driving. If you sense your child needs to talk, create an excuse to go for a drive together. This can be a particularly good environment for deep sharing because you have to look at the road, and your child feels less conspicuous. He still has your full attention without your eyes drilling into him (though in most circumstances you will want to be sure to look at your child while he talks). And this is a good time to talk without interruption.

A friend of mine has a daughter who calls often with many tales of woe. She keeps a basket of knitting close to the phone. By engaging her hands in a stress-relieving project it helps to keep her mind objective. It also gives an outlet for her emotions.

A significant aspect in successful listening will always be the dignity with which you handle the material your child reveals. When they erupt through the front door overwrought after a bike crash, don't laugh (as I once did). When they phone home with a broken heart from a fractured relationship, don't belittle their feelings (as my mother did). When they share a sordid story about their own misbehavior, don't faint or lecture (as every parent I know has done at least once). When you disapprove of the decision your child made, don't condemn. Practice a calm reaction, which allows your children to express fully their reasons and motivations and regrets. If we can be silent long enough, most of what we wish we could say will come out of our child's mouth instead of ours.

Our job as listener is to offer an audience, complete acceptance, emotional safety, and an environment of total trust. We then have the opportunity to demonstrate to our children the act of seeking God's wisdom as the only real solution to every problem or of rejoicing together and celebrating with God and our children when they have had a victorious experience.

If our children do not talk to us about the things on their hearts, what can we do now to change the pattern of communication? Family traditions and habits are always easier to establish while the children are still young, but sometimes we need to change directions and establish new habits in order to be a growing and improving parent. This is harder, but it can be done.

One thing you might do to show your child that you trust and respect him would be to share a confidence of your own with your child. Perhaps you are in the process of a difficult decision at work. Share your thoughts and questions at the supper table. Create an environment of sharing. You might feel awkward if you aren't in the habit of sharing that personally, but after you do it a few times it will come easier. Furthermore, you might be surprised and impressed at the suggestions your child might have for you. Later, be sure to share how the problem did or didn't work out.

Virginia's daughter attends a distant boarding school. The daughter often suffers bouts of low self-esteem, and Virginia has discovered special times alone with Dad will restore her soul. So, Virginia orchestrates opportunities for the daughter and Dad to take long drives together. Invariably these drives provide the atmosphere for sharing that benefits the entire family.

A father and son might attack a car repair activity together and turn it into a time of getting to know each other better. Look for ways to turn natural events into special occasions. Any time your child lets you peek inside his heart and mind, you have just experienced a very special occasion.

Another way to create an atmosphere of sharing might be to read a book aloud together that would open the thought processes and conversation to a deeper level of personal sharing. Read the book, and than ask questions at the end of each chapter that will encourage your child to open up and go beyond the surface of everyday life. Start easy, so that all of you get accustomed to sharing thoughts and questions before you broach the really tough stuff. Or a TV program might set the stage in a similar way. Just be sure to follow it with a period of discussion.

Children who respect their parents will want to know their thoughts on an important decision they must make. A child who knows he is respected will also feel much safer in opening his heart and life to his parent's scrutiny. So determine and practice the habit of respect. Then you will have much more opportunity for listening.

And trust me, once you start listening, you will never stop. There is no greater honor than to be able to share your children's hearts and minds as they learn and grow. My children are all across the hurdle into adulthood, but I still listen as much as ever. Last night my youngest son (the night owl) called me at 11:00, and we talked until 12:30 a.m. I felt rich and honored, even though the conversation was rough. And I loved him more than ever for the willingness to share so much of his heart with me. By listening often and deeply, we stay close in our hearts, despite the miles between us.

To look again at the Susie story, it's obvious to all of us that Mom made a mistake. It's also obvious that it's far too late to go back and let Susie share her achievement in the first flush of excitement. Of course

Mom will talk to Susie today as soon as she gets home from school and learn the story she missed yesterday.

But the important thing is to learn from our mistakes. What will Mom do tomorrow when Susie comes home from school? Perhaps she could make a point of being available without a telephone in hand whenever her family first arrives home from whatever activity they've been on. She could plan a 30-minute debriefing time as soon as Susie comes home from school or Bobby comes in from his ball game. Or she could practice dropping a plate. Would it have mattered if dinner had been five or 10 minutes later than planned? With knowledge of Susie's accomplishment, it might even have been turned into a celebration.

Listening enriches everyone's life. Give it a try.

Chapter 9

Framing
Family Worship

Recently my children and I discussed the ingredients of a strong family: unity and a sense of acceptance, common goals, the ability to stand alone comfortably. A family draws together to nourish and enrich each other and then lets each person fulfill his own potential.

But what is the forum that nurtures this unity and togetherness? I believe the most important routine of our own family togetherness has been a shared dinner table and a shared prayer circle. A dinner bringing each person to the table at the same time with absolutely no other purpose than to eat the meal, and the attention of each other can set the stage for open and interactive conversation. To follow this dinner table interaction with a time of family worship sets the tone for greater intimacy and deeper sharing. This family worship time can be unifying, it can be a battleground, or it can be an interruption tucked in the cracks between TV shows.

The boys, still sweaty from their play, sat on the floor with the basketball between them. Sis quickly said good-bye to her friend on the phone as the family gathered for worship at the end of the day. Daddy bowed his head and offered a simple, direct prayer before opening the Scriptures. He read only a few verses, then posed a question to the family. Responses rose from each of them to fill the room with opinions and more questions.

When Daddy felt satisfied that they had delved into verses deeply enough for a personal answer, he asked for each person's prayer request. One by one they went around the room and mentioned a need or situation that had arisen during the day and still awaited solution. Then they knelt together and each one prayed aloud, joining hands as well as hearts. As they finished praying, Mom led them in a prayerful song of commitment, and they concluded with a warm family embrace.

I sat entranced through the whole experience and vowed to create such a scenario for the family I would have of my own someday. I couldn't remember ever hearing anyone else in my house even praying aloud and could hardly imagine ever having a worship time like I had just witnessed.

A few years later I spent a weekend with another friend, thinking this might also be a home where family worship was part of the routine. I looked forward to having this shared family time. What a contrast!

After dinner, still seated at the table, Dad opened a book, commanding silence and hands in laps as he read a page out of the devotional book. When he finished, he didn't even look up, but bowed his head and murmured, "Joey, it's your turn to pray." Joey muttered a ritual prayer, and the family scattered.

Later I asked my friend if they had family worship every night. She laughed a cynical laugh and said, "Only when Dad's here. Isn't it awful? I don't know why it's such a big deal to him. At least it's short." And with that comment she changed the subject.

These two experiences happened many years ago and since then our family developed our own style of family worship. It has gone through many cycles of change and growth and monotony. In fact, I would have to say our family worship pretty accurately reflects my state of Christian experience. When I am having a "dry" spell in my ability to connect to heaven, our family worship becomes routine and dry as well. When I am in a time of growth and discovery, our family worship activities contain a fresher, more immediate interaction.

More recently our family decided to analyze the purpose and role of worship for today's families. It was a good exercise for us, for it wouldn't be too many years before the children would be conducting family worship for their own children. Our discoveries were quite basic.

Family worship is a time to connect spiritually with each other and to let the children see God as the Head of the household. Actually this will happen only if God is indeed the Head of the household. Some people go through the motions of worship without acknowledging God. Through personal experience I have learned that I can introduce my children only to the God I know personally. When I feel distant from God, I have a hard time showing Him as real to my children.

Earlier I told about the night I felt compelled to apologize to my children before I could lead out in family worship. When we take the time to prepare our hearts for worship, we and our children will benefit much more from the experience. To kneel in prayer with people you've just been yelling at is very difficult. That's why having worship follow the supper hour can be important. Supper gives you a chance to connect on a less intimate level and paves the way for a deeper level of intimacy during the worship time. If you can create an attitude of pleasant acceptance of each other during supper, it will be much easier to begin worship on the right note.

If quarrels do erupt just before time for worship, be creative in your manner of erasing their negative impact. And remember, the devil is at work and he will want to upset the tone of your worship experience. So be prepared to counter his efforts. Sometimes just singing a song or two can erase some of the dark shadows threatening to disrupt the mood of reverence and unity. Go around the circle and give each of your children a compliment, or have them each give the person on their left a compliment. Be alert to preparing your children for worship.

Family worship can also be a time of imparting your values to your children. Look for stories and books that teach your children the lessons important for their current age. And I urge you to generate and encourage conversation and participation in the family worship circle. Ask questions that cause your children to think beyond the surface, and then practice listening to each answer.

If we accomplish unity during the worship time, it has to be cultivated deliberately. It won't happen accidentally. This is a time when parents have to be wise and sensitive. Some quarrels are not easily resolved and take days instead of minutes. But when the time is right to solve the disagreement or strained relationship, make worship a place where people can be honest and open. By example, show them how to confess their wrongs to each other. And further, show them how to forgive each other. As hard as apologies can be, accepting them is sometimes even harder. It takes practice and example. Worship can create an atmosphere where it is safe to be open.

In another experience within a family circle, one of the children had taken money from the other children. It hurt. They felt betrayed and angry, yet they also were quick to forgive and understand. Peter was concerned that the offending child might not be held fully accountable for his actions and thus not as chastened as he ought to be in order to prevent a recurrence. So one night in family worship each of the children faced each other and told their sibling that he had hurt them, how they felt about it, and what they expected of him to correct the problem. It was a devastating and traumatic experience for all of them, but it allowed the erring person a basis of love and acceptance to admit his wrongs and discuss how the family could help him overcome the problem. Instead of accusations and emotional diatribes, they prayerfully and kindly put the problem in the open, holding the offender accountable for inappropriate behavior and then developing a plan to provide a family solution to one person's problem.

Without respect and love between all the family members, this could not have happened, and the outcome would not have been so productive. Through previous years of family worship Peter's family had developed a trust base and a safe place to be honest together. How different the outcome of such a severe crisis if the family worship format had not already been established. Anger, hurt, and defensiveness would have created barriers and lack of unity. Solutions would have been much more difficult.

Sometime during your own family worships, look up Webster's definition of worship. I'll not quote it here but look it up together and then in discussion with your children generate your own personal definition of worship. Doing an activity like this not only involves the whole family but helps to give new perspective to your experience.

A family I know well has discovered the joy of praising God. They begin their worships with a praise service. They share and recount all the divine interventions they can recall. Then they sing and pray aloud, telling God how much they love Him and all the reasons they praise and worship Him. Pretty hard to be morose and difficult after a sharing time like that.

But a different family I also know well orders the children to sit a certain way, no one on the floor, and to sit up straight, then reads a boring reading to which no one listens. The whole experience is concluded with a ritual prayer according to the checklist of whose turn it is to pray. They have absolutely not one word of personal conversation or any sense of praise, or even any sense of acceptance for each other. They've done their daily duty. Period.

I can't help but wonder how we as parents will be held accountable for the times we give our children a negative picture of God. No matter how noble our intentions, we must be very sure to present our Lord in an attractive way to our children. Our job is to demonstrate God's unconditional love and total acceptance of each child. The way we conduct family worship is part of that demonstration.

A decision to conduct family worship in your family will face many obstacles. The obstacle can be as simple as what direction or content the worship time should have or as complicated as how to find a time when all the family members can be present and without distraction. Worship with a deadline can be disruptive to mood or concentration. Perhaps some family members have deep-seated differences that create an atmosphere of hostility whenever all are in the same room.

Depending on the ages of the children, worship each evening with the entire family may not be possible. In the cases where teenaged children have jobs or after-school activities that make family schedules complicated, it might be easier to begin the worship practice on weekends. Friday evening worship was always a favorite in our household and rarely was missed even during the hectic teen years. Sabbath sundown worship was also a special time of reflection on the day we had just been through. And sometimes Sunday evening was our best time for worship because the weekend had wound down and the new week's activities had not yet intruded. So, if midweek times are too disruptive, try beginning with a regular time throughout the weekend. Meanwhile, examine the reasons midweek times are hectic. Can things be scheduled differently or could the TV be turned off earlier (or never turned on!).

A 13-year-old boy had gone to spend the day with a group of friends, but he felt quite anxious to be home by supper time Friday evening. He kept track of the time and made sure nothing happened to interfere with his return home. He loved being with his friends and thoroughly enjoyed the day's outing, but nothing in life could be better than Friday evening supper and the family worship that followed. Dad was often busy during the week and missed family worships, but on Friday night he was always there, and after supper was cleared away, the whole family would crawl into Mom and Dad's king sized bed for a time of reading and snuggling. This long-legged boy knew that nothing could be more fun or more important than an evening of family time in that king-sized bed.

Problems often will threaten the family worship commitment. One challenging situation will be what to do about unresolved conflicts between siblings or between a child and a parent. One suggestion might be to find a book about a similar experience and read it aloud together over a period of a week or more. Be sure to talk about each chapter as you read. When the book is finished, plan a time without a deadline or distraction and prepare some questions that will allow the differences to be aired. It might be well to have a tissue box handy and to be prepared for a few fireworks. Anything can happen during the process of resolution. Having all family members present and involved will help to dilute the intense emotions and create a bit of balance as the issues are discussed and resolved. Always conclude such a time with prayers and a song or two. It gives time for the Spirit of God to be renewed. It also puts a seal on the new sense of unity and acceptance.

The concept and practice of family worship begins as the couple first dates seriously. Can you pray together? Is it natural to share scriptures, and are you able to talk about what you have shared?

One young couple brought their first baby home from the hospital and stood together by his crib as they tucked him in that very first night together: a new family of three. They read a simple story of Jesus and prayed together. A visiting parent teased them, but they responded, "We do not want this child to be able to remember a time when we did not have family worship. If we start the first day, we won't have to wonder if we've reached the point of when his memory begins."

A good habit can be started at any age. Perhaps your family has not been in the habit of family worship. Perhaps your children are nearly grown and ready to build homes and families of their own. Even then is not too late for family worship. Show your children that you are willing to grow spiritually and that you can make positive changes in your own life. Then help them to be the couple that begins their life together based on the unity of Jesus and companionship with Him.

If we want our children to give us the respect to which we are due as their parent, we must show them how it is done. I have discovered that children who do not respect and esteem God rarely respect their parents. So by giving them the example of family worship, we show our children that God is worthy of our respect, and we demonstrate to them how they can also respect God.

By making family worship meaningful, interactive, and satisfying to our children, we also give them our respect. When we waste our children's time and make unrealistic demands, we have devalued them, and in return they will devalue us. So an inspiring family worship creates the true environment of mutual respect for the entire family, including the heavenly Father.

Chapter 10

Firm Foundation

For the second day in a row I found myself calming fussy children and playing peacemaker almost full-time. Of course, with two toddlers and a baby, our household rarely radiated peace and relaxation, but some days definitely felt smoother than these last two had been. Monday evening did arrive and finally all the children appeared to be asleep for the night. Whew!

Always the analyst, I tried to figure out what caused the sense of unrest and tension the children seemed to be wrestling the entire day and the day before. Naturally I expected them to be a bit restless and cranky on Sunday after the all-day outing we had on Sabbath, but this was two days later. I mentally reviewed the previous couple of weeks and thought I might be seeing a pattern.

After many days of observation and an awareness I hadn't previously activated, I learned that our Sabbath excursions cost at least three days or more of edginess and loss of control for the children. By the time things settled back into a comfortable routine and pleasant behavior, it was Sabbath again and we would be gone for the day. Meals, naps, and bedtimes all were rearranged, as well as the little rituals that fill a toddler's day.

And then there were four. With two toddlers and two babies, it became essential to maintain as even a keel as physically possible for these very active and sensitive little people.

For the weeks we could manage consecutive days of consistent meals, naps, bedtimes, stories, and bath times I found our home to be much more peaceful. The children's tempers were more relaxed. Their explosions of impatience and outbursts of hurt feelings occurred much further apart. Their ability to play together with laughter lasted for longer periods of time. Also, their tendency to fall asleep on schedule shortly after being tucked into bed for the night or for a nap improved. Meals became less of a battleground.

Many years have passed since those days of infants and preschoolers, but I have discovered that most people have a basic need of routine and schedule. I have noticed also that in their hectic whirlwinds many parents can be too quick to let their children's routines slip. A household with a consistent daily pattern gives the family members a sense of rhythm and self-control.

A child with insufficient sleep cannot handle his own emotions and will behave in an erratic fashion—with fits of temper at unusual times and bouts of unreasonable tears and frustration. Earlier we talked about the benefits of preventing naughty actions as the best means of discipline. So one of our children's most important tools for temper control is a daily schedule that continues to be consistent day after day after day. Failure to provide that basic foundation of self-control makes the parent share the guilt when a child loses control of his emotions and actions.

We can teach our children proper behavior much easier when we prepare them to be in control. An ingredient of providing security for children no mater what age is to let them know exactly when they will be expected to lie down for a nap or sit down for a meal. When will it be OK to play with neighbors, and when will I need to take a bath? What time is worship, and what order will we follow for bedtime rituals? With those items following day after day in a dependable routine, the child feels much safer and better equipped to handle life's myriad little frustrations.

It was a real surprise to me to learn that one of my children in particular truly could *not* go to sleep at night after a day of irregular naps and meals. Being extra tired actually lessened her ability to relax enough to fall asleep. This caused hours of crying and generated another day of out-of-control behavior. Before I understood and accepted this phenomenon, we had many hours of bedtime war. After I realized her very real difficulty, I redoubled my commitment to routine and changed my reactions to her inability to stay in bed. I played meditative music for her and rubbed her back and legs for long periods of time. I sang monotonous, comforting, little made-up tunes (I couldn't sing songs she knew, or she would join me). I recited Scriptures until I exhausted my memory, then started over. Sometimes this took hours, but the problem was mine, not hers. I had failed to provide her proper sleep hours the day before. I paid the price.

Young children have a reputation for bedtime rebellion. Actually, older children sometimes have the same problem. One of the most important ways to prevent this scenario is to create a list of nightly traditions, filled with comforting touches and lots of love.

For example, always start this routine at the same time every night—even if you have company. The children will know what to expect and will be far more apt to cooperate if they know what's going to happen and when it will happen. Always give them a warning before requesting that they cease their play. Make the warning age-appropriate. Five minutes to a young child is a long time. As you create family traditions, you might want to copy one I learned from my sister-in-law. Her grandchildren have a song that accompanies the picking up of toys. So the warning to interrupt their play comes in the form of Mommy singing the "pick-up song." Then they are less likely to fuss about putting their toys away while singing a peppy, lilting tune.

Our bedtime routine sometimes began with a bath and being sure the bedrooms were tidy, with all clothes tucked into the hamper. This was followed by tooth brushing and drinks.

Then we snuggled into one big chair and had stories and worship. After we prayed together, we would hug, kiss, and giggle. Then the children would make one last visit to the bathroom and get one more drink. (Since drinks were the choice excuse to get up again.) I then visited the children in their beds and took however many minutes necessary to chat and to tell them I loved them. We played a game and made "I love you" a special secret whispered in each other's ears so no one else could hear. I usually started with the youngest and ended with the oldest—or started with the boys and ended with the girls.

The most important part of this time is to make it feel unhurried, relaxed, and pleasant. Create an attitude of peace and specialness. The other element important for me to convey was the uniqueness of each child. This was a time to give individual attention to the life and thoughts of each one. In our house the children often were seen as a single unit because of their closeness in age, or it was easy to say "the big children" or "the babies." I tried to make sure that bedtime reminded each of them that I saw into their hearts and knew they weren't just a group.

Several people in my world of friendships are elementary school teachers. I also spent a period of time as a school board member and spent time in classrooms with my children and as a substitute teacher. I discovered a vast spread in the students who obviously had a regular and adequate bedtime. Some children came to school without breakfast in their tummies. The difference between those who came to school with sufficient sleep and a nutritious breakfast was visible. Those who came from a home with schedule and routine had the necessary tools to learn new things and also had much better skills getting along with their classmates.

A parent who cares about his child's grades and achievement, a parent who wants his child to be liked and content, needs to give him the platform of feeling good physically.

I have learned that including breakfast in my children's routines when they are young and adjusting to the revised schedule of school life gives them better fuel on which to function while they sit in the classroom. It also increases the likelihood they will include time for breakfast in their personal routines when they leave home for college or academy. Once children are accustomed to eating breakfast, they feel incomplete without it. If breakfast is sporadic and inadequate when children are growing up and learning life's habits, they rarely manage to find time to eat when they live on their own. Research has shown the importance of breakfast for good performance in the academic world—which begins in kindergarten.

Since my children were such active people from the earliest ages and also easily overstimulated, I learned a few little things that really help to maintain a peaceful home.

They played contentedly at home and filled many hours with creative and imaginative activities, but they also loved to go out, especially when it meant they would play with friends. Usually their excitement bounced back and forth between them until they became tightly wound little springs able to shoot to the ceiling without notice. When this mood over-took them, no one ate well at mealtime and I could not possibly expect a successful nap. I learned not to give them much time to anticipate outings. In the morning I did not mention a late-in-the-day change of routine until after all meals and naps were completed. At night, tucking them into bed, I did not speculate about the activities of the next day and didn't hold out promises of events far in the future.

Remember that children have a different time value than we adults do. Tomorrow can seem an eternity away to a preschooler.

Another important part in planning the family's day concerns outings to the grocery store or the mall. If you are pushing a shopping cart up and down grocery aisles when your child is normally sleeping or should be eating lunch, you are pushing a lit firecracker that could explode at any moment. As much as possible, plan these types of outings, which can be very stressful for both child and parent, when the child is at his best. Give him a chance to behave nicely, and both of you will be much happier. A well-rested and nonhungry child will accept correction of his wrong be-havior much more readily than one who is already feeling uncomfortable. It might be less convenient, but I found shopping late at night to be an al-ternative to shopping with stressed children.

As the children grew and progressed through their elementary years I discovered summer vacations to be especially challenging. After a rigid schedule of getting up and dressed and ready for school, followed by the evening routine of piano practice and chores, then bedtime, suddenly the day yawned vacantly before them. I did not have children that ever slept in past 6:00 a.m. until they were high schoolers.

While children absolutely need time to play without deadline and time to be carefree and unaware of artificial constraints, they also continue to need that firm foundation of routine. Without routine my children were much more apt to quarrel and to feel unreasonably grouchy and discontent.

So when they were all in grade school I invented the dreaded charts and lists. At the time I first put these charts on the refrigerator, the children truly believed I had to be the worst ogre that any child had ever endured. Later, they felt smug and proud of what they had done, but at the time they complained loudly and showed the charts to anyone who came to visit. I think they hoped that enough negative votes from my friends would discourage my expectations.

The daily list included a variety of things, from making their beds and brushing their teeth to performing one secret good deed without getting caught and a new memory verse every day. The weekly list included a variety of books to be read and a few specific chores to be done. Each evening we updated the charts with stickers; a certain number of stickers meant awards. As the years passed, the lists were updated appropriately until they included things like making a recipe for an entrée or a dessert and some recipes needed to be doubled, tripled, or halved. I tried to include things on the list that touched on each of their school subjects.

In our busy home the children's help with daily and weekly household tasks became essential. Summer or school year they were each responsible for some aspect of preventing total chaos. Washing dishes, making beds, emptying garbage were only the tasks of a beginner. As they grew they became better able to accomplish anything needed to provide an orderly household.

Chores that contribute to the efficiency and well-being of the entire family should be a part of every child's development. Children who participate in oiling the wheels of a smooth-running household have a greater sense of confidence and esteem. Doing a task that lightens someone else's load makes children feel good about themselves. The assurance that comes from doing a job well also enhances a child's self-image. I could not have managed without the assistance of my children, but I have learned since that they benefited even more than I did by their valuable contributions. Children like to feel important and like to be part of the team. A child whose parents wait on him often has a score of hidden or not-so-hidden insecurities.

One time my seventh-grade daughter visited a friend after school. While they watched supper preparations the friend's mother asked the friend to take the overflowing garbage outside. The girl made a face and refused to touch the garbage. My daughter was appalled. In our home the children had grown accustomed to feeling part of the family team and would have taken out the garbage without being asked—just because the bag was full. My daughter came home feeling proud of her contributions to our family and more determined to have a good attitude about helping the family.

Michael had a hard time doing dishes. He ignored his turn and found himself with a penalty of several extra days of dish duty in a row. He still tried to ignore the task. It would have been much easier for me to go into the kitchen and wash up the dishes, but in the end that would not have been fair for Michael or for the other children who had taken their turns and accomplished the job on time. By insisting that Michael wash the dishes and finish the job, I showed him that he was a person of value and was capable of doing a quality job.

In my house, while I was growing up, my mother often found it easier to do a job herself rather than struggling with disagreeable and uncooperative childish helpers. Consequently, when I married and established my own home, I had zero experience with many basic household tasks. I took quite a while before I felt competent as a homemaker and wife. I chose to spare my children that same struggle. They didn't always appreciate the education process, but knew they were expected to do their assigned tasks cheerfully, on time, and competently. Otherwise the same assignment would be on next week's list or even repeated the same day.

Allowing the children to do a poor job when they had the ability to do it better let them get away with being lesser-quality persons. So by insisting on a job well done, I insisted on high-quality children. Don't let your children settle for less than they are.

Regular schedules can be self-imposed when they aren't dictated by outside sources, and every family member benefits when schedules are set up and maintained. I don't mean to suggest that all spontaneous activity be shunned, but spontaneity always should burst from the basis of a routine life. Then we're equipped to survive the disruption. Also, if the bulk of your life flows through a schedule, your chores are more likely to be done, thus allowing you to participate in a spur-of-the-moment event.

My youngest son struggled with the concept of doing chores first and then playing. His normal manner was to putter and goof off until the phone call that I was on my way home from work. Then he tried to do a whole day's worth of chores in an hour. He rarely succeeded. But this quirk also meant he missed a few special opportunities because his "have-to-do's" weren't done, and he had to stay behind. A schedule gives you time to join your friends impulsively.

As a young adult I experienced migraine headaches. After visiting a variety of doctors, I wound up in a neurologist's office. Among other suggestions, he advised me to sleep the same hours every night of the week and to eat my meals at the same times every day. Sleep specialists recommend that their patients sleep the same hours every night for maximum rest and as a prevention of insomnia.

Maintaining a consistent sleep routine for young children can be a challenge for active parents who like to go out and have other involvements. I learned to hire a sitter and leave my children at home, even though it seemed costly and inconvenient. I was rewarded the next day with sweeter children than I would have had if I had kept them up late the night before. Yes, providing children a routine is a sacrifice, but the consequences for all the family are worth the cost.

Probably the best bonus from a life of routine is a greater sense of confidence and self-respect. A tired, cranky child does not feel confident, nor does he like himself very much. A child without self-respect doesn't really have the tools to offer parental respect. Further, a parent who respects his child's life will prepare him to cope by providing the foundation of adequate sleep and regular nutrition. Without fuel a child can't function well. With fuel, he has no limitations.

Build the foundation solidly, and the building will stand taller and straighter, and will last longer. Be sure your child has a strong foundation, and you will also have his full respect.

Chapter 11

Tackling Television

Saturday night, the highlight of my week. At 11 years old, I looked forward to Saturday night because it was the only night I could know my dad would be at home, and we always played games. Chinese Checkers. Sorry. Clue. We laughed and teased, and challenged each other. Dad worked seven days a week and rarely took time to play. He also rarely took time to interact with us children. I loved Saturday night.

Until the television appeared in our living room. We were not the first ones in the community to have one, but we certainly weren't the last either. That first Saturday night I remember vividly. The shock of actually having a TV! Then we sat down together to watch our first program: Gunsmoke. Wow! I went to bed reeling from the excitement and tensions of the program. But as I lay in bed that night, I realized we had not had one minute of conversation, and now I felt lonely.

After the arrival of the television, we no longer played games on Saturday night. We no longer teased and laughed around the table. Instead, we sat in the same room facing a talking box and didn't even speak to each other. When the last program ended, I had five minutes to say goodnight before the news came on, then it was back to "no talking." Looking back, I can see that I began to lose my sense of value to my father on that very first night of TV watching. In practice, the TV programs became more important than my thoughts and feelings. I felt in the way when I wanted to chat. My insecurities increased.

Many people have written against the programming on the television, suggested boycotts of certain stations, and demanded a variety of ratings. Though I do have personal concerns about the content of what's available on TV, I have greater concerns about the TV itself.

First of all, it unconsciously becomes more important than the people in our lives. The feelings I experienced as a child are still strong in my memory, and I absolutely do not want to give my children the same message.

I have to insert here a story which I wish I didn't have to relive. During a short time while the children were at the toddler and preschool stage, we bought a television, and I developed the habit of watching the evening sitcoms. Since my husband spent most evenings out visiting and attending meetings, it kept me company and gave me something to look forward to at the end of the day. Our family bedtime for the children had always been early since they woke up by 6:00 a.m. no matter when I tucked them in. A 6:00 p.m. night was the only way they could get enough sleep to function well. Most of the evening shows started at 7:00, so that gave me an hour to get the bedside chats finished and answer the final questions.

After having the TV for several weeks, I realized I missed the longer talks the children and I sometimes had as I made the tuck-in rounds. I found myself watching the time and hurrying to finish so I wouldn't miss anything on TV. I also showed zero tolerance for later interruptions after I had completed the bedtime performance. Anyone appearing at the end of the hall by the living room was summarily scooped up and hastily returned to bed with a scolding and no listening ear to determine if the appearance might have been for a legitimate need.

Finally, one night after I had been particularly impatient while being interrupted at an exciting moment during the TV program, I actually heard myself. And oh, how ashamed I felt! I punched the off button for the power and wept in agony. Somehow I had made a stupid TV program more important than my precious little children. Prior to this I had sometimes shared some very tender and private moments with a late night snuggle. How could any TV program compare with the loving arms of a chubby toddler, or a sleeping head on my shoulder while I sat in the rocking chair?

Looking back across the years, I do not remember a single scene from a TV program. But I do remember moments of shared love and conversation with a sleepy little person who needed some alone time with Mommy.

I share this shameful story in the hope that you won't make the same mistake I did. Don't make a TV program more important than the fleeting moments with your children. Don't hurry the chats that let you peek into your child's heart and soul. When you leave the TV off, you don't have to watch the clock and shorten their stories.

Second, TV watching becomes an easy escape. Creative play and productive activities fall by the wayside when we switch the TV on. Consequently, self-worth is further diminished because there's no sense of accomplishment or achievement.

One Christmas vacation the children and I decided to rent a VCR and borrow my parent's little TV set. At that time we did not have a television set of our own. Since we had spent money renting the VCR, we decided we should watch lots of movies to get our money's worth. After two days with too much movie watching, one of the girls commented, "I feel like a mush brain. I don't want to watch any more TV even if we do waste our money. Better to waste our money than our brains."

Occasionally we go through a spate of excessive watching and always someone refers to Shari's "mush-brain" comment. Our children and I have discovered we simply like ourselves better when we avoid TV watching as a lifestyle.

Third is the matter of the family schedule. In the previous chapter we talked about how to include family worship in the daily routine. Well, personal experience has told me that engaging in a meaningful family worship is not possible immediately after turning the TV off. The excitement, fast pace, and entertainment of TV is completely counter to a spell of Bible study, which is a contemplative, introspective activity. Additionally, having a satisfying caliber of worship is also difficult while you watch the clock in anticipation of the coming program you want to see. For our family, television directly blocks evening worship.

And that goes for meals around the dinner table, too. Many people I know now do not even try to eat as a family sitting together at the table, but the ones who do often fill their plates and then sit in front of a television set. Family interaction is quite limited as all of them sit facing away from each other. And true communication is hampered when it has to be squeezed in during commercials. To have a progressive level of sharing when it comes in brief tidbits is not easy.

But the worst aspect that undermines the family value of mutual respect comes from the programming itself. Even on commercials husbands and fathers are often treated as buffoons. Children are smarter than their parents and are rewarded for humiliating them. The cutest, most appealing star roles for children are often filled with sharp wit and scenarios of kids outsmarting adults. Ever wonder why school teachers have such a problem commanding respect in the classroom? They have a room full of youngsters who all watched Bart Simpson last night.

Many families find it easiest to control the television set by not having one at all. But for those who have decided to have a set in their homes and who want to maintain a rein on the amount of viewing time, I have a few suggestions I've collected from various people through the years.

Accompany your TV set with a VCR. The best use of a VCR is the ability to decide on your own which hours you will spend watching TV. When you have selected a program you want to share with your family, record it. Then watch it together at your own convenience.

That brings up the next point. Watch programs together as a family. Don't use the TV as a babysitter, for a variety of reasons, the most important one being that you won't know what your child has seen or how he has reacted to what he has seen. Make watching TV an interactive and shared experience.

After the program ends, turn the TV off and talk about each person's reactions to it. What feelings did it evoke? Why? Does it make you want to do something different in your life? What did you learn?

Take a few minutes each week with the programming schedule, and decide in advance which programs you will watch for this week. Then record them and watch only the shows you have planned to see. This puts you in control rather than the TV's being in control of you.

When TVs and VCRs first became popular, all the parties and get-to-gethers my children attended began to be movie watching instead of game playing. My children would come home feeling cheated. With movies, we have no interaction and social connections are stunted. How do you get to know someone new by looking at a box across the room? My children much preferred the laughter and sharing of playing a game to the laziness of watching movies. Movies were isolating and passive. They attended social functions to be with people.

Again, it's a matter of making others feel important and valuable. Treating people with respect means listening to them and interacting with them. Movies rob people of that chance to share at a personal level. To get beyond the polite niceties and create enough comfort for a person to open his mind and heart takes time. When we're busy watching other stories, we have a harder time giving each other enough attention.

Several years ago when my husband pastored a small church, one of the mothers came to our home. She felt frustrated because her teenage sons did not like Sabbath. Later we visited in their home, and I began to understand the boys' inability to enjoy the Sabbath hours. The television set blared and performed its antics every waking hour—until one minute before sundown on Friday evening. And it was turned back on immediately after sundown on Sabbath evening.

Meals were eaten in front of the TV. Conversation was at a minimum. No one had to entertain himself, because other entertainment dominated all their senses. Of course Sabbath felt boring to them. It was quiet. It didn't move around. It required a more active participation than they were accustomed to.

An older friend commented to me when I was a young adult, "People are afraid of their thoughts these days. They seem to want music or TV sets filling every available moment. It takes away the thinking time."

I've pondered that statement from time to time. We do need thinking time in order to be balanced, complete people. We also need thinking time to have a chance to hear what God might be trying to tell us. And we certainly need quiet time to think and to listen when our children decide they want to talk to us. People without TVs often do a much better job of communicating with each other.

I believe a quiet household gives our children a higher sense of value and a better quality preparation to cope with their own lives. Now is the time for Christian parents to decide that it's OK not to have a TV available to our children. Someday they will thank you for the gift of "quality time" and peace that you have given them.

Chapter 12

Raising Readers

Third-grade parent-teacher conference for Krista. "Well, Mrs. Wolcott, it appears Krista struggles a bit with her math skills. All the rest of her grades are excellent, but the math grade is a C minus."

I knew she was capable of a better grade and pondered aloud to the teacher, "I suppose she's just having a harder adjustment to copying her own problems down now that she's outgrown those workbooks." Her small muscle coordination had been slower to develop than the other children's, and consequently handwritten skills were a bit of a struggle.

The teacher agreed, and we began to talk of other things. As the meeting drew to a close I asked to see Krista's desk and went over to take a look at its contents and her projects. While there, I noticed it was directly next to the classroom library shelves. When I lifted the lid to peek inside I discovered a generous stack of additional "outside" reading books. I commented to the teacher, "I think we just found the solution to Krista's math problem. Try moving her desk, and see what happens. Krista loves to read more than anything else and I guess she's reading during math time."

Few people I know love books and reading more than Krista does. As she grew we learned that she was not able to lay a book aside at the end of a chapter. Whenever she was called to do something, her standard response became "when I finish this chapter." But we later would find her well into the next chapter.

Books became a part of our family identity. We read entire books aloud long after the children read well on their own. We read together and created memories and family bonds that can be attributed only to shared experiences. We often had two books under way, plus whatever each of the children might be reading. On Friday nights, especially in the winter months, we sometimes read an entire book aloud in one evening.

For me, reading was simply something I loved to do. Therefore, I enjoyed sharing the activity with my children. From the earliest baby days into teen years, reading was a time of intimacy and snuggling. Troubled days ended with comforting quiet times. The voice itself soothed and calmed as we read. Reading was a time of discovery and adventure. Books became treasures.

I learned later that children who spend time with books and stories have many educational advantages. Not only are their vocabularies and language skills expanded, but so are their ideas. Reading teaches a child to think. It exercises the brain by modeling how a thought is developed and explored.

A very young child begins to identify that the parent is reading something other than the pictures and consequently is prepared for letters to turn into words and words into sentences and sentences into stories. A child who has been read to will also have a more concrete grasp of language and proper sentence structure. Occasionally let your finger trace the words as you say them aloud, and the child will understand the relationship of words to the telling of the story.

Recently I spent a couple of weeks helping a young family while the mother endured a period of bed rest during her second pregnancy. The first child, age about 20 months, and I spent a lot of time reading and playing together. I readily confess I initially anticipated reading books with Sierra just for the pleasure of holding her on my lap while we read. As I read each book several times I had the privilege of hearing Sierra "read" her first book to herself. She, of course, had memorized the story from hearing her mommy and others read it to her many times, but she felt the satisfaction of knowing all the words (there weren't very many, and they were repetitious) and turning the pages herself and pointing to all the right pictures.

Then a few days later I had the thrill of tucking her into bed and being told "I love you" in response to another book we shared. I had forgotten that books and little people could be so much fun.

Another fun thing with Sierra and books came as she sat in her little rocking chair next to the bookshelf and chose books, not always familiar ones, and "read" them to her dolly. Many of the words were simply sounds, but she definitely had the idea of storytelling.

This brings to mind one of my niece's favorite sayings. "Only boring people get bored." She always carries a book under her arm to ensure it never happens to her. In so doing she travels to many new and unfamiliar places. She meets many kinds of people and spends time in all sorts of families. In real life she eagerly embraces a wide variety of new experiences and situations. Reading books has given her the confidence and mental preparation to meet new friends and go to unusual places.

A lower-grade teacher told me the other day that children who start school with a family background of reading aloud are culturally more prepared for the social adjustment of school. Reading exposes children to a wider variety of lifestyles and types of families than what they themselves live. These children are more prepared to accept differences of other students in the classroom and are more accepting of people in general.

Almost all of our children's school and learning experiences involve books and words. When we teach them to enjoy reading and to enjoy being read to, we give them a gift that no one can ever take away from them. We also give them a much stronger chance of success in the classroom throughout their school experiences.

At a recent family get-together my adult siblings began sharing a list of their favorite authors. We talked for nearly an hour sharing descriptions of the books each of us had read and why we liked that book or that author. The children sat nearby watching our enthusiasm for reading—even when we don't have to. Checking further, we observed that almost all of us had a book along with us, though we knew we'd all be talking too much to be apt to take a book break.

So as a family we demonstrated our zest for reading, traveling, and exploring. Our children saw an example of books in an everyday setting. We didn't just tell them to "Go read a book" as if to say "Get lost." We showed them the fun and joy of reading and then sharing what we've read.

Another way we used books in our family was as a means of developing a personal value system. I used the stories of other people to demonstrate the values I felt were important. In doing so, we had lots of fun reading about other families. One book that stands out in my memory is the book *Roll of Thunder, Hear My Cry,* which tells of a black sharecropper family and the trials they endured. The children began identifying with different characters and assigning each other roles. It allowed some excellent conversation and sharing.

By letting books and other people's stories present the values we want for our children, we can avoid many lectures. The illustration of someone else's experience will be far more impressive than any "sermon" a parent can muster. It also means that our children don't feel threatened, accused, or defensive.

I also discovered teachers like for new kindergarteners and first graders to be experienced with reading together because children accustomed to listening to stories being read aloud are more inclined to know how to sit still in a classroom setting. Reading gives the body a chance to be still while the mind stays active.

As my preschoolers began to outgrow afternoon naps, I still required an hour of quiet time every day. They could choose one book to read or look at during this quiet time—thus developing their own daily habit of reading to themselves.

This can be an excellent preparation for a daily personal devotional experience for children. Children who don't enjoy reading have a more difficult time finding satisfaction or motivation to develop the lifestyle of Bible study and reading of devotional literature. When we give our children the love of reading, we prepare them to enjoy a reading time with God. Of course people who don't read much can still spend time with God. But I have discovered that it's easier for those of us who love to read.

When my children were old enough to read competently on their own, they also thought they were old enough to make their own decisions about what they should read. I learned to trade books with other parents and friends who regularly updated their personal collections. And we made frequent family trips to the library. Each child had his own card and took a book bag or backpack to bring our "haul" home.

As my children continued to choose many new books to read, I suggested categories for them to include on a weekly basis. I know they read some books I wouldn't have chosen, but I tried to downplay those choices and continue to flood them with the types of books I approved. The required reading topics included one biography, one nature story, one mission story, and one book about history.

In order to convince the children to open a particular book I thought they should read, I became a bit devious. I would read one or two chapters aloud until I came to a particularly exciting point. Then I would leave the book available for them to pick up and finish. The book quietly traveled from room to room as each of the children read it, thinking they were sneaking it away from me. I tried to ignore its absence and would begin reading a different book aloud a few days later.

We did have to develop a few rules about reading each other's books. Whoever received a book as a gift had first rights. The others couldn't read the new book until the owner had time to read it first. Another rule that had to be enforced quite often: Once someone started a book, no one else could pick it up and begin reading it.

Since our whole family consists of competitive people, we often kept lists of what books each person had read. So occasionally I selected a book and asked a series of questions to ensure it had actually been read before it counted on the list or could be turned into school for a book report. Only once did I expose an unread book, and that child was so mortified I doubt she ever again claimed to have read a book that she hadn't.

A close friend recently married a woman with nearly-grown children. She commented to me that she had never met anyone who read books as avidly as her new husband, but she wished she had married him earlier because none of her children liked to read, and none could imagine attending college. They just hadn't developed any interest in books and learning. Primarily they played or expected to be entertained. As for the mother, she sat down only if there was a TV program to watch. She thought it seemed restful to see her husband sitting in the evening with a book on his lap.

When we give our children the love of reading the pleasure of books, we give them an opportunity to explore the world. But we give them also an inner confidence that really can't be measured, another accomplishment to enhance self-respect and to benefit the entire family.

By raising our children to be readers, we are raising them to personal achievement and contentment. By continuing to read together even as they grow, we are continuing to develop a series of bonds through shared experiences and time spent together. Thus we create an environment of harmony and peace within our homes, the very atmosphere of mutual respect.

Chapter 13

Mastering Manners

Think for a minute about some of the children in your neighborhood, church, or other social circle. Not your own children, but the children of another family. Which children do you most enjoy being around? The well-behaved, mannerly ones, or the out-of-control brats? Easy answer. Even little brats aren't much fun to be around.

Which of the children do you think like themselves the best? Again, easy answer. Brats know they are brats and don't much like to be around themselves either.

Next scenario. Your boss has invited your whole family to a formal meal in his new home. How will you feel about your children's table manners as they sit at his table eating unfamiliar foods?

The time to prepare your children to sit at your boss's table (or any one else's table, including your own) is today. If you wait for the big invitation and think you can cram a few manners in your children's minds, you will create a whole family of nervous wrecks who can't possibly enjoy the meal. The children will be sure to forget something, and they will be edgy. You won't have the confidence they can handle themselves, so you will be watching and ready to glare, frown, or shrink from embarrassment when they do forget themselves.

Today's frantic families and TV supper settings have taken a serious toll on the daily table manners of most children as well as their parents. Sitting down together every evening around a table is the most important step in developing children's ability to eat appropriately. Looking at each other and talking together makes modeling the behavior you wish to cultivate in your children much easier for you.

Then you can add a game and offer a reward when each child goes seven or 10 evenings straight without a faux pas. The habit of good table manners can be easily developed if you give it consistent reinforcement and some positive feedback. I recall my older sister learning the appropriate niceties in handling herself at the table. To catch her making a mistake so she would have to start her 10 meals over again was a challenge to all of us. But the pleasure of her special dinner in a nice restaurant alone with our dad made the reward worth the effort. It also motivated the rest of us to want to emulate her feat.

Some people believe that "fancy" table manners are no longer in style or necessary. That certainly seems to be true in many cases. But those who make the decision to teach their children these old-fashioned manners also choose to prepare their children for all sorts of situations. Again, it comes back to giving a child the inner confidence to handle himself in unfamiliar territory. For a person with the habit of good manners, the ability to share a table with any type of setting allows that person to concentrate on the people at the table rather than to be nervous about his own actions and focused on himself.

A couple years ago I read a newspaper article about a woman giving classes in manners to grade school children. She didn't start out with that plan, but it just sort of happened when her friends learned about her commitment to teaching those manners to her own children. Many parents evidently hadn't really learned the appropriate way to handle formal situations and fancy meals when they lived at home, so they didn't have the tools to teach their own children. Through referrals from friends and friends of friends, this woman had developed a business more than three years earlier.

I recall her overall assessment of the need as being one of basic respect. By teaching children how to behave properly, you also taught them self-respect and respect for the people around them. A child who knows the proper way to meet people, the way to act at a table, whether formal or informal, and the appropriate way to speak to others can handle new situations more confidently than the unmannered person. This training also teaches the child to concentrate on the person being met instead of being distracted with his own shortcomings.

My children were too old when I read about this woman's manners class, but I found myself wishing I could have sent them. Teaching children to behave just right is hard work, and I knew I had let down on that one.

Since then I have visited people who have taught their children to address their elders with "sir," "ma'am," or "madam" and to rise to their feet and offer a chair when an older person enters the room. We feel good to be around people who are polite. And I've been embarrassed when my healthy, able son sprawls in the most comfortable seat of the room while and older person sits on a kitchen chair, the floor, or a stone hearth.

As a single parent, I find it is sometimes awkward to teach a child to respect me. One time we spent a weekend with some special relatives. As we arrived, several different little things occurred. Our hosts made sure that I, the mom, had the best bath towel. They made sure I had the most comfortable seat at the table. I was given the best bed. Each time the hosts pointed out that "the mom deserves this." I didn't need all that attention, but it made a strong point to my children about the respect they also owed me. I later felt grateful to my cousins for that simple reinforcement.

I also found that we help each other in the training of our children in many ways. We have friends in our social group who are the only family with very young children. Invariably, when one of the little ones does something naughty, the nonparents find it easy to laugh or giggle. One of the children kept making rude noises, and it wasn't long until half the adults were also making those same rude noises. Big oops! We need to help each other raise polite children, not aggravate the challenge for our friends. We also need to help the children in our sphere of influence to develop a strong respect for their own parents. Beware of reinforcing the wrong behavior, however innocent our response might feel. Decide to be supportive of the parents' values and to look for ways to act on that decision.

While I was visiting some friends, their 3-year-old grandson was staying with them. At suppertime my friend pulled some especially pretty paper plates and matching napkins out of the cupboard. Little Jaden instantly exclaimed, "Oh, Grandma, tank you!" Her face lit up, and she responded warmly to him. He had a huge amount of positive feedback for his natural words and will probably be sure to say those words again. Grandma's smile and hug felt good to him. Whatever time his mother spent to teach him to say those simple words will be repaid over and over. It made the child a delight to watch and be near. And it made Grandma very proud as well.

One of the first ways to teach a child to be courteous is when you allow her to answer the telephone. Many people let children too young to take a message or use the phone properly to answer calls routinely. On the other hand, a child with a pleasant telephone voice and polite phrases leaves a delightful feeling in my heart. These lessons can be taught quite easily when a child feels grown-up enough to be able to answer the phone. A few role-playing sessions, and your child will feel good about the accomplishment. Your friends will enjoy the results too. Remind your child that the telephone is often the first contact someone will have with your family and that the speaker represents everyone in the household.

Many little things combine to make a person seem polite and a joy to be around. I just learned that many youngsters do not even know it is impolite to wear a hat indoors, especially at the table. Lifting a hat or tipping a hat when he meets a lady is probably expecting far too much. A gentleman will always stand when he greets someone older or a woman of any age. This will seem an automatic way to teach children to honor their parents and grandparents when we teach them to do these little actions.

The courteous phrases should become automatic. The pleases, thank-yous, ma'ams, and sirs should flow readily in conversation. Good manners can overcome a host of other deficiencies. The story of the renowned surgeon, Ben Carson, comes to mind. As a child, he lived in humble circumstances, but by adopting the refinements of the educated, he learned to fit into any situation and to have the confidence to face it. Knowing proper manners prepares a person to deal with unfamiliar situations in a safe and acceptable fashion.

Teaching a child to look someone in the eye whenever they are in conversation is another important habit. One of my children had a hard time learning to look at people while they spoke with him and it caused a bit of awkwardness because he was deemed unthoughtful when he was really quite a sensitive person. Lack of eye contact suggests lack of trustworthiness.

Teaching our children to speak graciously and to honor other people gives them a large measure of respect from those same people in return for their words and actions. When we give the effort to teaching our children these skills, we really give them a lifetime of courtesy from others. Perhaps it's time to resurrect those manners classes and teach them in our churches, schools, and homes—and make them a daily habit for ourselves. It's time to make manners automatic and spontaneous.

Chapter 14

Parents

Parenting

Becky and Jim brought their new daughter home from the hospital and pronounced her "queen of the house." All of us understood completely because we had shared their difficult quest for a child. When Baby Julie whimpered, both parents rushed to comfort her. No unpleasantness would ever touch their precious baby.

Their attention was admirable and "cute" while Julie was an infant, but by the time she was 4 years old, the novelty wore off and most of us found their fawning over this pampered child a bit obnoxious. We'd forgotten the long years of waiting her birth, and wondered if the spoiled "queen" would ever be allowed to live a normal life.

A variation of this story is evident in many homes as children become the focal point around which parents perform. It is particularly evident in homes where both parents work and feel guilty about their many absences. They seek to atone for their absence through gifts and antics meant only to seek their child's acceptance and forgiveness. The child soon learns he holds the power and is quick to learn how to exploit that power. Tired and guilty parents can easily miss the manipulations and intelligence of their children. They give in to the child's demands in order to keep peace in a harried household.

I can remember standing firm against my adolescent daughter—she hated me, and my heart ached more than I could have described. I questioned myself over and over and wondered if I should back down. I felt alone and bereft. As a single parent, I felt especially in need of my children's love and acceptance. It was a real struggle every time I had to make a stand for something out of harmony with my children's requests.

In retrospect, they now thank me for doing what felt very hard to do at the time of emotional trauma. But that doesn't help anyone while going through the experience.

A couple things to keep in mind for the hard days: Children *need* parents to act like parents and to take a stand on things involving family principles. When children are allowed to "rule the roost," the parent isn't on duty, and that's too much responsibility for any child.

Another point to remember is that parents and children cannot always be best friends. Peers and nonparents can be their friends, but parents *must* be parents.

I once read the counsel to "choose your battles." I heartily agree. Everything can become a war zone, and then home is a battlefield instead of a haven. Determine to preserve the atmosphere of heaven; learn to ignore the small stuff, and choose beforehand which things will be intractable. The more sure you are of yourselves as parents, the more confident your children will be as children. A wavering, hesitant parent gives children and teenagers a shaky foundation to launch them into adulthood. By standing firm on a few specific issues, you also give your children the courage and strength to stand firm.

Several months ago a young man who stayed in my home for a few weeks shared his frustration at being an only child in a single-parent household. I listened and asked probing questions about how a lone parent should handle the family balance, especially with only one child.

He felt smothered. All his mother's attention lay upon him and it weighed him down. I laughingly said that everyone ought to have four children. No way can you concentrate that hard on any one of them! However, I imagine my children also have felt that sense of weight from being the focus of attention when they would have preferred some privacy to figure out who they wanted to be and how they could manage the transition into adulthood.

I doubt that there are any easy or right answers to this dilemma. To find the balance and to remain firmly in the parent role will always be a struggle. Developing friendships and supporters who know you and your family helps. You need friends who will listen when you need to talk and will help you see the situation more objectively when your child "hates" you and wants to run away.

I recall the night, though not the reason, three of my children had driven me to the edge of sanity (and probably off the cliff onto the other side), and I locked them out of the house. They trooped down the street to a friend's house—adult friend, my friend—and returned with sleeping bags, prepared to spend the night in the yard. They were great little martyrs to a tyrant mother. I don't even remember now whether they spent the night in the yard or not, but I do know that outside intervention provided perspective and time for emotions to relax.

All families need that perspective and objectivity from time to time. Emotions nearly always cloud the facts of the situation and distort the real issue. Since we are a family with five strong-willed people, stubbornness could sometimes also be a deterrent to amicable resolution of issues.

All children need total and complete unconditional love, but they also need parents to stand firmly as heads of the household. We should let them be carefree as children ought to be, yet provide boundaries within which they can be safe and happy. As they grow and mature, those boundaries will change, and sometimes those changes occur with a bit of struggle and pain. But boundaries too tight are better than no boundaries at all. Children are good at pushing the boundary edges occasionally, just to be sure the fences are still in place, not because they need to be removed. And we parents need the wisdom of heaven to respond to those nudges.

Jesus promises wisdom to all who request it. Pray the prayer of James 1:5 and you will find it easier to be confident in heading your family.

Many communities and churches separate children according to age groups. This is a practice I don't encourage. Our family developed many friendships with other families and frequently went on outings in family groups. This enhances a variety of strengths and enriches everyone involved.

As teenagers, my children counted several adults among their circle of friends. This provided them alternative sources of comfort and advice in times of distress or perplexing transitions. At times when they needed someone outside the family to provide sounding boards, they had a selection of personalities to sit down and talk things over with.

Also, since my children lived in a household without a father, these family group activities provided them with a variety of adult male friends to mentor and befriend them. They also offered the children examples of healthy marriages and man/woman interaction. Many times at sunset on Sabbath evenings, one of the men in the group would lead out in sundown worship. This gave opportunity for my children to see men in leadership positions in the family circle.

Another strength is that the children learned to befriend and communicate with "peers" of all ages. They played with children much younger than themselves and became role models and mentors to these younger ones. They had older friends to help guide them through the growing-up stuff. They had adult and grandma friendships that felt natural and comfortable.

Children who associate primarily with age-segregated outings feel less confident when faced with a younger or older person than the usual group. Leadership and follower roles are more often assigned as labels, whereas in a mixed-age group, the leadership usually transfers, depending on the activity. Older children playing with younger children learn patience, tolerance, and gentleness. Younger children playing with older children get chances to practice some more "grown-up" skills before they become essential. Children mixing with adults learn to participate in real conversation and to think thoughts they might not otherwise think.

Family group outings also give support to a family struggling to maintain the parent as head of a single-parent household. The children observe their parent as an equal with other parents and see the other parents being parents to their own children, so they are more accepting of the parental actions at home.

Being a child in today's world is not easy, but we can make it easier for our children if we let them be children—carefree and safe for as long as possible.

Chapter 15

Establishing Esteem for Educators

Teacher Sands shook her head and wrote a failing grade at the top of the paper. Another book report about an unread book. It really wasn't typical for this student, but inability to leave an assignment blank must have prompted her to falsify the report. Mrs. Sands sighed and wrote a note beside the grade. "Please come and talk with me."

After the meeting with the fourth-grade teacher the tearful student took the paper and slunk back to her desk, shame emanating throughout her whole body. She seemed sure the disgrace was written in bold letters across her back for everyone in class to see. She didn't quite fit in with the popular girls and always marched about a half step behind. She longed to be accepted and to be perfect.

One day later Mrs. Sands had an unexpected visit from the errant student's irate mother. "How dare you accuse my child of cheating or lying! She has never in her life told even one little falsehood and I know she wouldn't have written a report about a book she hadn't read." The woman continued to rant to Mrs. Sands, "you're just trying to put her down and embarrass her in front of her friends."

Mrs. Sands tried to calm the distraught mother and suggested she read the child's report and the book it should have represented. Indignant, the mother marched out of the room and took her child with her for a "day of mental-health recovery."

Another parent recalled the day she received an invitation to meet with the principal about her son's disrespectful behavior. He had called the principal an unsavory and demeaning name. The parent cringed in telling me the story. She commented, "My gut reaction was to feel guilty and ashamed. I dreaded facing the principal whom I liked and admired." I shared her humiliation.

Remembering some of my children's varied antics and my difficulty in separating my own ego and self-image from their naughty actions, I completely identified with the feelings my friend described.

What happened to the days when a child disciplined at school would arrive home to be doubly punished for his misdeeds in the classroom? What changes have taken place that make parents so defensive of their children that teachers sometimes have their careers destroyed by a vindictive parent on behalf of a child who really does need to be disciplined and corrected for inappropriate behavior?

When the first of my children entered formal education in the classroom of Miss Willis, a third-year teacher with 20 years worth of wisdom, she and I often visited and discussed the adjustment of my children to the classroom. In one conversation, she shared her philosophy (and that of many teachers before her): "If you believe only 10 percent of what the children tell you about my classroom, I promise to believe only 10 percent of what they tell me about your home." We laughed together and agreed the adage represented good advice for both parents and teachers.

As my children traveled through the classrooms and hallways of grade school and then academy, many of their teachers became family friends. I tried to visit the classrooms often, and I usually invited the teachers to a meal in our home at least once early in the school year. Because my children were close in age, I had an advantage few other parents had. I heard several versions of the same story and learned to be a little more objective. Children can be quite passionate about a perceived injustice. But their passions can also cool quite quickly. When the parent may still be upset and protective, the child may already have put the problem to rest.

While on a school tour in academy, one of my children had to be sent home for violation of tour rules. As long as I live I will remember that day, and so will the children who remained home and spent it with me! I paced and muttered and proclaimed as I waited for her arrival home. Fortunately, by the time we were reunited, I had calmed considerably and had regained a bit of common sense and perspective.

I learned several things from this experience:

One, I learned that parents are never prepared for their children to make major mistakes and public fools of themselves.

Two, I learned that the first reaction is almost always one of embarrassment for both myself and for my child.

Three, whatever action the teacher or person in charge takes is usually slightly different than what I would have done to handle the same situation.

Four, my next reaction is usually one of anger toward the child for being so stupid, when certainly he does know how to behave more sensibly.

Five, now I need to help my child find a way to mend fences and restore the broken relationship—which can be done only when I put my pride out of the way and separate myself from my child's life.

My youngest child, Michael, often quipped playfully whenever he did something "stinkery," "You made me this way." At the time I was really annoyed when he would say that. However, later I came to realize it was good for me because it made me realize I had done my best to "make him different" but he had resisted my efforts and chosen a divergent path at least pertaining to that particular mannerism or behavior.

Every classroom situation is unique, and some teachers probably will treat your child in other ways than you think he ought to be treated, but I urge all parents seriously to analyze their own role teaching the children to respect every teacher. Lack of respect in the classroom is a permeating problem in every school today and parents need to align themselves with the teachers in order to give the children every opportunity to grow into responsible citizens.

The fourth-grade student who lied on her book report and then couldn't admit the truth to her mother was allowed to get away with dishonest action because the mother was too ashamed to hold the child accountable.

In reality, the relationship between the girl and her mother was damaged. And it made the child uncomfortable whenever her mother and the teacher needed to interact. Had the mother taken the time (always difficult to find when you work full time and try to cope with children and a home), she would have realized her daughter had indeed cheated on the schoolwork. Then the mother would have felt supportive of the teacher and could have helped the daughter to face her own inability to "be perfect."

Recently a junior high teacher discovered drugs in the possession of one of his students. He said he had personally observed money and the packet change hands between two of his students. When the parents became involved, they were immediately defensive and claimed it had to be a mistake. Now they are fighting the school to avoid the students' expulsion. The teacher feels undermined and discouraged. Facing the truth of the children's possessing drugs, the parents would be more likely to get the help now while the children are still impressionable and perhaps avoid bigger problems in future years. Instead, the children have parents denying the truth and a teacher feeling he's in the wrong job.

One parent related the time he received word that his son had become involved in a major theft on campus. Heartbroken, the parent called the school and asked, "What is my role in this? What can I do? How do I handle this?"

The dean wisely advised, "Love your child, and help him repent and accept the consequences." I offer this as excellent advice for all of us parents.

I assure you that at least once, each of your children will make an immature decision resulting in some sort of discipline from a teacher or school official. Please give yourself time to react and think before letting your emotions take over and make you as much a part of the problem as the child. Determine to be part of the solution and part of your child's accountability rather than being in denial and becoming defensive. Our children are separate beings from us, and though they do reflect on us as parents, they also are individuals with decisions and consequences of their own for those decisions.

Remember Michael's mocking "You made me this way" and realize our best attempts may often be overridden by the child's impulsive whims.

If you do sense a problem in the classroom, be slow to act and thorough to research it. First, accept that you will not love every teacher, and neither will your child. With respect for the teacher as a basic attitude, you can live with most less-than-desirable situations. Our children are far more resilient than we often think they are. We cannot protect them from every unpleasantness, and sometimes helping them learn to cope with difficult experiences is giving them opportunity for real personal growth and skills for the rest of their lives.

I urge every parent to spend time in the classroom whenever possible, getting to know the teacher as a person, and learn to let emotions pass before creating confrontations. Even if you feel the punishment or disciplinary action is unfair or unreasonable, remember that life is not always fair, and it's beneficial for your child to learn that lesson. Usually he's not hurt by the event.

Teachers teach because they have a heart for children, and to do the best job possible for each child they need respect from each child's parents. We should make a committed and obvious effort to show our children that we value and honor their teachers. Many parents make a point of giving a gift to the teacher at Christmas, on a birthday, or other event. Some of us may even choose to give these gifts because we want to express our support and encouragement directly to the teacher. However, the most important recipient of this gift may be the child who witnesses and participates in the expression of honor toward the teacher.

Yes, some teachers don't measure up, but as parents, we should choose to be vocally and actively aligned with the teachers in order for our child to gain the greatest benefit from his school experience. Respect for teachers begins with the parents. Respect for teachers is essential to our child's development and preparation for life. Respect for teachers is an inheritance every parent can give his child.

Another way to help foster achievement in the classroom and enhance the learning time is to speak positively about school activities. One parent talked loudly and often about her own inability to master mathematics and times tables, so how could she expect her child to do well? The teacher believed the child capable of better performance, but lack of support from home undermined the teacher's attempts to give the child positive self-esteem about math skills.

It could just as easily be science or spelling. Whatever our personal scholarly weaknesses, we should do our best to give our children every advantage by giving them a positive state of mind about learning and about school.

If we hated school we should not admit it now to our children. A reluctant child can learn to feel better about going to school when the parents project more enthusiasm for the opportunity for learning. Reading together and sharing a love of learning will help your child want to learn, too. Prepare for school by getting a special outfit for the first day, buying a new book bag, or planning lunch treats. Figure out what motivates your child, and make a point of using that motivation to help the child feel good about school. Your involvement will always be the best support you can give both your child and his teacher.

As I have said, most teachers teach school because they love children and they love to watch them learn. Do your best to see them as allies in your child's journey toward adulthood and responsible citizenship. Everyone wins when children and their parents hold the teachers in high esteem.

Chapter 16

Honorable Parents

I f you were to ask a Christian parent to define his goals for his children, the answer probably would include living forever with his children and Jesus together in the new world. And we have a promise how such a desire can be fulfilled.

"Honor your father and your mother, so that you may live long in the land the Lord your God is giving you" (Exodus 20:12, NIV).

As a parent, giving this promise to our children has three basic ingredients.

Do we honor our own parents, the grandparents of our children? Honoring them is probably fairly easy in the early years of our own parenthood. But as our children grow up, our parents grow old. And the challenge to honor our parents in their diminishing years becomes more obvious.

Honoring our aging parents becomes both a decision and a commitment. It also includes forgiving them of any perceived or real failures we feel we received from them during our formative years. The danger of carrying grudges against our imperfect parents is greater to those of us who carry the bad feeling than it is to the one we hold it against. Over years it becomes a poison, and slowly that poison seeps into our heart and hardens it in many ways. That hardening can also separate us from God and from the ability to conduct our own lives in the way we want to live. So forgiveness for any wrong we feel has been done to us is essential for our own mental and spiritual health. Sometimes this forgiveness will have to be offered in the form of a letter to a now-deceased parent. Even though they can't see the letter, writing it will be good for us. This will free us to offer an attitude of respect for our children's grandparents.

The decision to honor a parent also involves actions to express that honor. I have heard an absent parent tell a child how much he has loved the child through the years the child did not see or hear from him. No one can feel loved without receiving some expressions of that love. I always tell people that love is a most active verb. So is honor. Love might mean doing something we really don't feel like doing, and doing it not out of duty but out of affection. Our children will witness our true attitude, so if it is duty, they will identify that motivation probably even before we ourselves can recognize it. Children are amazingly perceptive, especially when things in our lives don't ring true.

Jody's father is an alcoholic. He's been an abusive and manipulative person for as long as Jody can remember. She doesn't particularly even like this man who is her father. He certainly has never been an honorable person to her. He is now an old man and in need of care, but Jody resents his needs and intrusions into her life. However, she wants to be a responsible person and to be a true Christian. She has struggled many hours in prayer on this issue.

Today, her father is in a nearby care facility where Jody monitors his treatment and attends to his business affairs. It's not a pleasant or easy situation, but she feels at peace to some extent. Her behavior is honorable even if she doesn't feel it in her heart. This is honor in action if not in affection. I admire Jody's commitment to honor her father whether he deserves it or not. It certainly epitomizes the grace God offers to us, though we don't deserve it.

Recently my adult children gave me the gift of honor. I wanted to help a friend do a yard project, so I asked my children if they would consider spending a day with me working in my friend's yard. I doubt any of them really wanted to spend their day in that manner, but all of them came, and we worked together for a productive, pleasant time together. I felt blessed and reassured of their commitment to me, and my friend now has a beautiful yard and a warmed heart.

Honoring our parents also means speaking of them with the proper amount of respect and not belittling them as their aging behavior would sometimes make it easy to do.

A cousin-in-law gave a beautiful example. Duane spoke up and commented that his wife's parents held his eternal gratitude and respect for the person they had raised his wife to be. Because he valued and treasured the qualities in his wife, he also valued the people who gave her those traits. He spoke with such eloquence and gentleness that I was deeply touched by the esteem he gave these people, who can sometimes be very difficult.

This reminds me of the time my son was entering the mid-teens and the difficult mood swings that accompanied that transition time. On the worst days I would remember the chubby toddler throwing his moist, pudgy arms around my neck and telling me he loved me as he snuggled down for a turn on my lap while I sat in the rocking chair. By remembering the special moments, I could continue to love and treasure this tormented boy-almost-man time of challenge. Perhaps the same applies to our parents. If we can recall the reasons we value them, that will make it easier to get through the hard times.

Three years ago my father died after he broke his hip in a fall. He suffered from Alzheimer's disease and went through some very difficult times prior to his death. Some days he was angry and stubborn, completely intractable, and impossible to manage. But now, as the children and I reminisce about him, we recall the gentle side of him, and we recount the funny affectionate moments: his excitement over Christmas, his pride in his children and grandchildren. Remembering the good moments can help sustain love and respect during the tough times.

The next important ingredient in teaching our children to honor their parents is first to teach them to value life beyond their own. When a child lives in a self-centered, undisciplined world, he cannot honor other people because he's too busy thinking about himself. Remember Becky and Jim from Chapter 14? As they catered to little Julie's every whim, they taught her to think of herself more than of her parents or other family members. We need to teach our children to see the bigger picture. As they recognize the hand of God in the existence of all that lives they will learn to give God's creatures greater value and respect. As they learn to control their own impulses to misbehave they will think of how others feel. As they learn to contribute to the household they begin to see the bigger picture and where they fit into that picture.

A small child sees Mommy and Daddy in the place of God—another reason why the parents being the head of the household rather than letting the child rule the kingdom is so important. As a little child learns to respect Mommy and Daddy he also begins to learn how to respect God. He will first love and honor those whom he can touch and see and hear. Later our children will be able to act out their respect for us only because they first have a respect for God, who will enable them to love and honor us as we diminish in age and ability.

This brings us to the next and most important ingredient. We must be a parent our children finds honorable.

I suppose the definition of an honorable parent would be a person who lived the values he talked. For example, if you don't want to take a phone call at this moment, don't ask your children to lie about your presence. Instead, it would be best for them simply to take a message. Or do you conceal certain types of income when you figure your taxes?

Another example reminds me of the grade school student who forgot her permission slip on field trip day. She simply stated that she'd forgotten to bring the required paper. Her teacher seemed surprised that the girl offered no excuse or suggested no blame onto someone else (*i.e.*, "My mom didn't sign it"). I laughingly asked someone who he would blame for lost tools when no children were still living at home. Listen to yourself (or those around you), and discover how often people instinctively point a finger of blame toward someone else rather than to state simply, "I failed to do it" and take responsibility for their own actions.

Being honorable doesn't require perfection, but it does require honesty. I remember one parent explaining that a parent must never admit to a child when he did something wrong. I was appalled. Children are quite smart and they are quick to spot hypocrisy. We are wiser to quickly admit our failing and apologize rather than to pretend we did nothing wrong. We fool no one except maybe ourselves. To give our children an example of how to say "I'm sorry" is to give a positive witness.

I heard a story of grandparents of a divorced couple telling one of the children various faults of the "other" parent. Today those children have a hard time honoring the grandparents who undermined their family unit.

Children of divorce have a special challenge in learning to honor their parents. Often they get caught in a crossfire of criticism between the parents or are the victims of desertion as one parent leaves the area to build a new life and is rarely seen. It might take them years to sort out all the confusion and come to a point of honor. Or they might discover that absence of a parent creates a void in the father or mother category of parenthood. And where love and honor might have been, there is nothing.

Any person who seeks to come between a child and his parents or to break down the parent/child relationship in any way commits an act against the commandments of God. As Christians, we need to do all we can to teach respect and honor, combined with forgiveness toward all children and their parents.

Criticism, gossip, and intolerance for the faults of other people around us also contribute to an environment where respect might fail to thrive. An adult who continually finds reasons to be discontented teaches his children also to be discontented and to find fault—or else it can alienate a child because he, too, will feel that measuring up to his parent's unachievable standard is impossible. When we express acceptance of imperfect people in our community, we make it much easier for our children to accept us. A parent who frequently criticizes a child's teacher creates a situation where the child will lose respect not only for the teacher but also for the parent. This almost always works both ways. Remember the grandparents who criticized the parent? Well, rather than diminishing respect for the parent in question, the grandparents lost much more.

Parents are human and apt to make many mistakes along the way of life, so I suggest again: It is not the specific mistake as much as how we respond to the mistake that is the real issue. Do our children see us seek forgiveness from God? Do they see us lean on His power and strength? Do they see us seek the presence of the Holy Spirit in our hearts? Have they watched us grow in the grace of Jesus?

We can give our children the gift of eternal life by becoming parents who can be honored and by teaching our children how to give honor and love.

I want to live in heaven with Jesus and each of my children. What else could possibly be more important? And I hope you and each of your children will join us there. In the meantime, let's commit ourselves to developing the atmosphere of heaven in our homes.

In an era of blatant disrespect all around us, may we, as children of the heavenly Father, find a haven of peace in the love and respect of our own families.